PALGRAVE POCKET CONSULTANTS

Palgrave Pocket Consultants are concise, authoritative guides that provide action-able solutions to specific, high-level business problems that would otherwise drive you or your company to employ a consultant. Written for aspiring middle-to-senior managers working across business at any scale, they offer solutions to the most cutting-edge issues across modern business. Be your own expert and have the advice you need at your fingertips.

Available now:

ATTRACTING AND RETAINING TALENT
Tim Baker

CONVERSATIONS AT WORK
Tim Baker and Aubrey Warren

MYTH-BUSTING CHINA'S NUMBERS
Matthew Crabbe

RISKY BUSINESS IN CHINA
Jeremy Gordon

THE NEW CHINESE TRAVELER
Gary Bowerman

THE WORKPLACE COMMUNITY
Ian Gee and Matthew Hanwell

PEOPLE DATA
Tine Huus

Forthcoming titles:

MAKING SOCIAL TECHNOLOGIES WORK
Ronan Gruenbaum

MANAGING ONLINE REPUTATION
Charlie Pownall

CRISIS MANAGEMENT
Alex Singleton

CREATING A RESILIENT WORKFORCE
Ivan Robertson and Cary Cooper

Series ISBN 9781137396792

About the Author

David Wolf is Managing Director of Allison+Partners' Global China Practice. Recognized as a leader in China's public relations industry, David specializes in helping clients manage complex communications challenges, including government relations, crisis, new market entry, and corporate reorganization. His current clients include Underwriters' Laboratories (UL), Micron Technologies, Airbnb, the Public Interest Registry, and the Canola Council of Canada.

In addition, David is called upon by regional and global media as an analyst and commentator on business in China, and contributes to publications including *Foreign Policy*, *The Holmes Report*, *EuroBiz*, *Media*, *Ad Age* magazine, and WARC. David is an editorial advisor for the *China Economic Quarterly*, and has been a blogger for eleven years at Silicon Hutong (http://siliconhutong.com) and *The Peking Review* (www.pekingreview.com).

Prior to joining Allison+Partners, David spent seven years as President and Chief Executive Officer of Wolf Group Asia (WGA), a Beijing-based strategic corporate communications advisory firm. Serving clients including Discovery Networks, Motorola Mobility, Google, Foxconn, Blizzard, AOL, About.com and Irdeto, WGA won both client and industry accolades.

Before starting at WGA in 2005, David led the Asia-Pacific Technology Practice for Burson-Marsteller, leading a team of nearly

50 professionals in offices across Asia and Australia. Prior to joining Burson-Marsteller, David was Managing Director and Chief Operating Officer of Claydon Gescher Associates (CGA), a boutique strategy and public affairs consultancy based in Beijing with a focus on media, entertainment, and telecommunications.

David has lived in China since 1995, and now divides his time between Beijing and Los Angeles. He holds a Masters degree in International Management from the Thunderbird School of Global Management, and a Bachelor's degree in International Relations from the University of California, Davis.

Building and Defending your Brand in the PRC

Public Relations in China

David Wolf

palgrave
macmillan

First published 2015 by
PALGRAVE MACMILLAN

Palgrave Macmillan in the UK is an imprint of Macmillan Publishers Limited, registered in England, company number 785998, of Houndmills, Basingstoke, Hampshire RG21 6XS.

Palgrave Macmillan in the US is a division of St Martin's Press LLC, 175 Fifth Avenue, New York, NY 10010.

Palgrave Macmillan is the global academic imprint of the above companies and has companies and representatives throughout the world.

Palgrave® and Macmillan® are registered trademarks in the United States, the United Kingdom, Europe and other countries.

ISBN 978-1-137-48379-9   ISBN 978-1-137-48381-2 (eBook)
DOI 10.1057/9781137483812

This book is printed on paper suitable for recycling and made from fully managed and sustained forest sources. Logging, pulping and manufacturing processes are expected to conform to the environmental regulations of the country of origin.

A catalogue record for this book is available from the British Library.

Library of Congress Cataloging-in-Publication Data
Wolf, David (Economist)
Public relations in China: building and defending your brand in the PRC / David Wolf, Managing Director of Global China Practice, Allison+Partners. pages cm. — (Palgrave pocket consultants)
ISBN 978–1–137–48379–9
1. Public relations—China.   2. Social media—Political aspects—China.   3. China—Politics and government—21st century.   I. Title.
HD59.6.C6W65 2015
659.20951—dc23   2015014437

Typeset by MPS Limited, Chennai, India.

To my parents, Valeria Jane Overman Wolf and David Wolf, Sr., who set my mind questing and my feet toward China.

To my in-laws, Cai Hong and Sun Yushu, who opened their hearts and home, allowing me to live a Chinese life from the inside.

To my son, Aaron Joshua Sun Zilong Wolf, who reminds me each day why what I do is important.

And to my wife, Tong "Sunny" Sun, who wove together the threads of my life and is my co-author in all things.

Contents

Acknowledgments

The cover of a book carries the name of a single author, but there is always a legion of people hidden behind that name who have given of their time and passion to contribute to the project. This book is no exception.

But I want to use this not simply to thank people who helped me, but also to call your attention to individuals who are outstanding in their fields in the hope that you might find their knowledge helpful.

First are two women who poured the foundation for my career in PR. Jeanne-Marie Claydon-Gescher, OBE, brought me into this industry in the first place when she hired me to join her Beijing-based government relations firm. Jeanne-Marie has an instinctive feel for the winds moving Chinese policy and regulation unmatched among those who watch Beijing's opaque politics. Susan Tomsett recruited me into Burson-Marsteller China and the world of "mainstream" public relations. She schooled me in the broad scope of the PR craft beyond the world of government. It is no exaggeration to say that this book would not exist without their patient mentoring, and much of their wisdom pervades this book. I have given credit to each as often as I could.

Scott Kronick, the long-time leader of Ogilvy PR in China, has been both a competitor and a friend, and it was his client referral on a cool November day that gave my little boutique strategy agency the wings to fly. His perspective and counsel have been invaluable. Jim McGregor at APCO has also been a source of counsel and clients. Jim has made the written word his profession, and his encouragement at key times has ensured that I continue my effort to pass what I know to a wider audience. Ye Yu of Hill & Knowlton and Eric Li at Naspers taught me more in two years about the way the Chinese government worked than a prior decade of study and experience had done.

Scribes like Jonathan Landreth, Kaiser Kuo, Jeremy Goldkorn, and Matthew Pottinger have been generous with their time and their feedback over the years.

My family has no better friends than Carolyn Wu and Joshua Kurtzig, whose unique combination of warmth, brilliance, and encouragement helped drive my work at critical points.

My colleagues at Allison+Partners, especially Scott Allison, Andy Hardie-Brown, Scott Pansky, David Schneider, and Bill Adams, supported this project from the outset, and Jerry Zhu, Richard Zhang, Jacky Jiang, Sophie Shu, Grace Song, and their teams shouldered the load when writing pushed work aside.

All of my clients have been supportive throughout, especially Ann Allyn, Angela Dansby, Natalie Harrison, Nanette Jiang, Bruce Jowett, Lauren Price, and Joyce Wang. There can be no greater statement about the importance of this book than the support they have given to it.

David Kelly, Philippa Kelly, and Amanda Rasmussen at China Policy have given me the luxury of working with some of the best minds on government in China, and their work on China's "New Normal" echoes and reinforces the understanding of China's changing business environment that pervades this book.

During the writing of this book I spent over half the time on the road, mostly in Beijing and Shanghai. An incredible legion of people at Marriott Hotels, China High-Speed Rail, Cathay Pacific and All-Nippon Airways made it possible for me to get out of my nook and write this book where the action was happening.

A wise author always saves the most important people for the end.

Author, editor, and explorer Steven Schwankert has been my writing coach and the "third hand" on my keyboard for a decade and a half. I could not have asked for a better writing mentor.

The team at Palgrave-Macmillan: Tasmine O'Riordan squired the project from the beginning, when Howard French brought me to Palgrave's attention; Stephen Partridge had the thankless job of editing this down to a manageable size: be assured that this is readable because of him. Josephine Taylor made sure that the relationship between author, editor, publisher, and marketer all worked, even when I was a dozen time-zones distant and trying to balance work, family, and the challenges of authorship.

Last and most of all, my wife, Sunny, keeps me grounded, builds me the headspace I need to write, puts up with month-long business trips, and provides the impetus for this work. She is my partner in everything I do and has helped me frame much of my thinking throughout my career, so while the blame for any mistakes or omissions are mine, her name belongs on the front of this book as much as my own.

Introduction

Introduction

Over three decades of experience have revealed three truisms about public relations in China that any executive must remember, whether you are in general management, marketing, or in a public relations (PR) specific position:

1. If you do business in China, either as an enterprise or an organization, you need public relations.
2. In fact, public relations is necessary in China to a greater degree than in any other market in the world.
3. Enterprises and organizations from outside of China may not need good public relations right away, but eventually they all need it, and they need effective PR more than their local competitors.

Why PR has always been important in China

Effective public relations has been essential for companies and organizations in the PRC (People's Republic of China) since Deng Xiaoping opened the country to outside investment in 1978. And yet, public relations has never been more important to success in China than it is today.

When Deng began the historic reforms that made China the economic miracle of the century and a lodestone for opportunistic companies from around the world, he ensured that words like "foreign" and "business" were no longer the obscenities they had been for a quarter century. What he could not do was end the residual suspicion and distrust of foreign enterprise instilled in the nation and its bureaucracy by decades of propaganda, nor could he (or would he) teach the Chinese people which brands were worthy of their trust and custom. Both of those efforts would require the time, patience, and careful cultivation of China's government and the public at large by the companies themselves – in short, persistent and effective public relations.

As China developed and opened to the outside world, companies began to face new problems. Early entrants paid heavily to pry open a new market, only to see their hard-won positions threatened by an inrush of opportunistic competitors. Later arrivals were vexed by a market that showed herd-like favor to market leaders yet so lacked any kind of brand loyalty that companies could watch their market positions evaporate in a matter of months. Niche markets were hard to locate in China's vast and opaque consumer landscape, and advertising went from non-existent to exorbitant seemingly overnight. Regulators created national standards and other regulations that seemed to focus on undermining the most successful companies. Consumers began taking their product and service complaints directly to the media, who then inflated each complaint into a systematic attempt to cheat the Chinese people. Every issue became a crisis, and every crisis represented an existential threat to a company's business in China. And all the while local companies, in particular state-owned enterprises (SOEs), seemed to be immune from the fray.

For the first 35 years following Deng's reforming and opening, this was the environment that companies faced: an enticing but intensely challenging market where hard-won success could be lost overnight for the most prosaic of reasons. Little wonder that proactive public relations became a hallmark of the most successful companies in China.

Why PR is more important than ever in China

Since 2013, however, the environment has changed. In the wake of the global financial crisis and the arrival of China's fifth generation of national leaders, it has never been more difficult to establish, build, defend, or rejuvenate a brand or corporate reputation in China. There are several reasons why this is the case, and why the "Happy Time" for companies is over in China.

Consumers are tougher: First, the consumer has changed. No longer the naifs who would buy a product and trust it merely because it sported a foreign brand, in the space of a single generation China's consumers have gone from being relatively unworldly and credulous to sophisticated and cynical. As a group, consumers in China have been bombarded by advertising and in-your-face marketing to such a degree and for so long that all but the very best campaigns are ignored, forgotten, or, worse, serve only to frustrate consumers.

Advertising is expensive: There are no longer any real advertising bargains in China: the media have become adept at pricing access to their audiences, and in the face of high and growing demand, rarely discount anything worth having. China's leading online portals charge for advertising neither by views nor by clicks, but by how many minutes and seconds your advertising is on the landing page. CCTV (China Central Television) holds an annual televised public auction each November, selling off the most worthwhile chunks of advertising time to bidders who hike the price of a five-second spot on the nightly news to Super Bowl prices. Few companies can still afford to rely on paid media to carry the primary weight of a marketing plan in China.

Competition is intensifying: Even before the global financial crisis, China was one of the world's most dynamic markets for a broad range of industries. In every industry, players from around the world flocked to China for a piece of the market, and in doing so ran headlong into a cohort of local companies in each of those markets that were equally intent on dominating in China ... and then going overseas to win over the traditional markets of the world's largest players. The result is that in nearly every industry each company faces a wider array of competition than anywhere else in the world, and a far greater challenge to stand out from the crowd.

Government is ambivalent: Beijing once welcomed foreign businesses as sources of capital investment, technical know-how, best business practices, and high technology that would serve as catalysts for China's economic development. Today, China has no shortage of capital, has a massive pool of technical know-how, a generation of business leaders trained in global best practices, and is managing to get hold of high technology far more easily than in the past. The global financial crisis was a self-inflicted wound in China's image of the West as wise, knowing, and capable, and a drumbeat of stories about ethical lapses at huge foreign firms make Multinational corporations (MNCs) appear deceptive, if not downright evil. This decline in the stature of the outside world, combined with China's apparent growth from success to success, has left the nation's leaders skeptical of the value of continuing to allow foreign enterprises to prosper in China at the "expense" of local competitors. A long and growing sequence of government investigations targeting the most profitable foreign companies offers unmistakable testimony to this change in attitude.

The challenge is not limited to foreign enterprises. Local firms, especially hard-charging entrepreneurs, find that they are facing a policy environment that implicitly favors the large enterprise over the small and the state-owned over the private. The internet offers some striking examples: online search leader Baidu is feted by China's national leaders even as the Party attempts to build a government-owned rival; online video providers are hit with onerous regulatory hoops designed to protect state-owned broadcasters; Alibaba is forced to restructure its ownership of its online payment subsidiary in a move to protect the business of domestic banks; and a local entrepreneur is denied permission to test-fly and certify a revolutionary electric aircraft in China, while a state-owned entity is given full government assistance and cooperation.

Nationalism is deepening: In the face of growing domestic political and economic challenges, Beijing is carefully stoking nationalism among the population and in business circles as a means of sustaining support for the government and the party. The spirit of China's accession to the World Trade Organization (WTO) in 2001 has been slowly whittled away in a spate of technical barriers to trade in industries as varied as agriculture and high technology. Business has become a new playing field in China's effort to extend the nation's commercial power around the world.

The mass market is breaking down: The myth of China as a market of a billion consumers has proven hard to kill off, but China's real promise for most companies will be realized as the nation evolves into a land of very large niche markets. As enticing as these markets are, mass media will be poorly suited to reach them, and the means of doing so among business and industrial customers is just as confounding.

China moves the Street: How a company and its brands, products, and services are perceived in China is no longer important *only* in China. China is now a real market for a large number of companies, and for a growing cohort of firms it is perhaps the single most important market on Earth. The Street knows this, and that includes everyone from large institutional investors to the punters who watch Jim Cramer on CNBC. News in China tends to hit the wires between noon and 6:00pm local time, which means that it is at the top of the ticker in the morning for every market across Europe and North America from the DAX to the COMEX. What a reporter writes about a company in China is, for reasons of both timing and attention, market-moving news.

This formidable array of challenges indicates that now, more than ever before, the degree to which a company is seen to play a positive role in China's development, the degree to which Chinese publics believe they can trust a company to serve more than its own selfish interests, and the degree to which a company is perceived as an indelible part of the future success of the nation, its companies, and the people are what determine a company's prospects in the China market.

Given all of this, you would think that the value of public relations would be widely recognized by companies and business leaders in China. For some companies – and we will talk about many of them in these pages – it is. But for each company that makes effective use of PR in China, there are three that do not, and often at critical junctures. The ratio is even higher in Chinese companies, many of which have leaders with strong technical and sales backgrounds who still see public relations as a regrettable evil rather than a potential source of competitive advantage. Indeed, as I once put it in a discussion with executives from a US video game company, "in the eyes of far too many of China's business leaders, 'branding' means getting a new logo, 'marketing' means buying ads on CCTV, and 'PR' stands for 'pay the reporter.[1]'"

What this means to you

The new era we are entering in China makes it clear that this attitude has outlived its usefulness to an enterprise interested in continued success in the world's largest market. Against a sea of challenges, making and shipping great products or delivering a reliable service is no longer enough. Companies must earn the right every day to enter or continue to operate in the Chinese market. A failure to play a positive role in China, become an indispensable part of the country's future, and to demonstrate that a company is worthy of trust leaves that firm vulnerable to the first issue or crisis that casts the firm in a negative light.

Public relations must be strategic, proactive, and consistent. It must address all of a company's stakeholders in China without forgetting that there are others from overseas who are paying attention as well. And PR must be executed with the same care, enthusiasm, and senior-level attention that a company gives to its sales, finances, and product development. As China becomes increasingly important to the prospects of our global businesses, a failure to pay due attention to the sensibilities of Chinese publics represents an existential danger to our companies.

How to use this book

I have written this book for the following people: those who are operating a company in China; those who are planning a new venture into China; those who are about to take on leadership of a China operation; those who oversee or are part of a global PR function; those who are supervising a China PR team; those who are new to PR, to China, or to both; or those whose company is just starting to develop an interest in China and is looking for answers on how to succeed. If you fall into one or more of these groups, or just have an interest in how PR determines success in China, this book is for you. While I have aimed it primarily at the foreign enterprise in China, there is much here to inform public relations people working in and for Chinese enterprises and non-governmental organizations (NGOs) operating in the PRC as well.

I will not spend a lot of time explaining the rudiments of public relations beyond what is absolutely necessary to underscore the differences between PR in China and PR elsewhere. Instead, I will focus on three areas:

1. How to avoid the hazards that have hampered the PR efforts – and the business success – of companies in the PRC.
2. How to build your China-specfic PR toolkit – the way in which the sum of approaches, tactics, and techniques that make PR an effective craft needs to be modified, trimmed, or augmented to drive organizational success in the PRC.
3. How to organize your PR effort and integrate it into your corporate structure and strategy in China.

Here is how I suggest you read this book:

If you are a practicing PR professional, I suggest you read it from cover to cover.

If you are an executive who is not a PR specialist but who is running or overseeing an operation in China, read Chapters 1, 2, 4, 5, and 8.

If you are facing a crisis in China right now and need help, read Chapters 3, 5, 6, and 2, in that order.

If you are a newcomer to PR who is seeking a PR position in or related to China, or you are a student with an interest in PR in China, read from cover to cover – while this is not a textbook per se, you will find all of this information useful.

Everyone else should feel free to read through the chapters in sequence, as to the greatest degree possible I have tried to arrange the book so that each chapter builds on the last to provide a comprehensive overview.

A few conventions

Finally, before we get started, a few notes on conventions used in this book.

First, the Chinese language is transliterated into roman-character languages like English using a number of different forms. The common method of transliteration used in mainland China today and the one we will use in this book is the *hanyu pinyin* system, the one that transliterates the name of China's capital city as "Beijing" rather than the previous "Peking."

Second, I will frequently use the word "foreign" in this context to refer to individuals and institutions from outside of China. This is a common practice in China, even among expats (who of course refer to *other* expats as foreigners, never themselves), and after much rumination on the subject I have decided to leave it this way, if for no other reason than to offer a subliminal introduction to the way the market thinks. A "foreign journalist" or "foreign correspondent" is therefore a journalist from outside of China; a "foreign company" is a company either with its headquarters (HQ) outside of China, or a company started by a non-Chinese inside of China; and a "foreigner" is simply an individual who is not a Chinese citizen. Throughout this book (unless otherwise noted) the term is meant to be descriptive rather than pejorative, so any offense is unintended.

Third, this book focuses on public relations in the People's Republic of China, and the terms "China," "PRC," "the Middle Kingdom," and the like will be used interchangeably to refer to the cities and provinces of the Chinese mainland along with the island of Hainan. Hong Kong, Macau, and Taiwan are for historical reasons each unique public relations environments of their own, and for simplicity's sake we will not address them here.

Fourth, to the greatest extent possible, I will try to break up large bodies of text. Naturally, I hope you take the time to read every word in this book, but the point here is for you to gain the information you need to think through your PR needs in China, plan them, and execute them. I provide lots of lists and bullet points that are designed to help you skim when you are pressed for time, and go back and read if you want more depth and clarification.

Finally, the focus in this book is on creating effective public relations, and I will use that term frequently. If it comes across as a little pedantic, it is because a depressingly large percentage of the public relations efforts in China seem to be conducted for the sake of doing PR, rather than for the sake of advancing a company's business and shoring up barriers to competition and other external threats. The latter is the only public relations worth doing, and it is the focus of this book.

Okay, let's get started. If you're not in the middle of a crisis right now, turn to Chapter 1.

1

The Basics and First Steps

If you spend some time strolling along the high streets of Beijing or Shanghai, you might think that most companies have China cracked: international brands are predominant among the cars on the streets, among the products in grocery stores, and in the advertising that pervades urban life in China. And you won't walk far before realizing that Starbucks, McDonald's, KFC, and Pizza Hut are daily staples of Chinese life.

But behind all of that apparent success is a struggle that preoccupies business leaders in China, yet never seems to make the headlines. It is the struggle to make those brands known to hundreds of millions of people while ensuring that decades of sweat and investment do not disappear because of a single misstep or act of hubris. Success in China is precarious, hard to obtain, and harder to sustain. It is a constant tightrope walk, and public relations has become the essential balancing pole.

Unfortunately, the vast majority of enterprises and adventurers who have sought fortunes in China have returned empty-handed, or worse. For each notable success, there are many more examples of companies that have given up or that have struggled mightily for underwhelming returns. While a range of factors can make the difference between success and failure, far too many companies in China fail – or, in many more cases, find their businesses permanently handicapped – because of fundamental errors in public relations.

At the same time, each company that enjoys lasting success in China has discovered that one of the critical keys is the need to build, nurture, and defend their reputation among the full expanse of important audiences (or "publics"). They learn that sales will move your product, marketing will convey its attributes, advertising will imprint the image of your brand indelibly in the minds of millions, and having lunch with the Minister of Industry and Information Technology will demonstrate that you understand the importance of *guanxi*[1]. But they also realize that none of those things will be sufficient in the long run.

China changes with a speed that makes Silicon Valley seem like Brigadoon, and keeping even core audiences happy there has vexed some of the world's smartest companies. Tastes change. New competitors (even local companies) pop up with a cheaper version of what you have to offer. A local competitor starts pouring poisonous disinformation about you into the ears of customers. Your advertising becomes a background drone. And your best friends in government are transferred, retire, die, or even get sacked for malfeasance.

The brutal truth in the People's Republic of China (PRC) is that regardless of how great your company is, how superb its products are, and how long you have been operating there, lasting success hinges on your company staying relevant for, and engaged with, a host of publics. That means winning over a lot of people, and doing so constantly and consistently. In short, success in China means having strategic and effective public relations. And "strategic and effective" is the key.

Every week companies approach me and my team with requests to "do their PR [public relations] in China," but a surprising number believe that "PR in China" means translating and distributing their press release. For some, that may be all that they really want: they have no intention of doing business in China, but somebody in their organization took a look at a draft release and growled, "Make sure this gets seen in China, too." For those companies, the best route is to work with a service like PR Newswire (PRN): for a few hundred dollars, they'll do a reasonably good (though not always perfect) translation of your release, and through their local China joint venture they'll send it out to dozens or even hundreds of relevant outlets. PRN will make sure that the release goes out and gets run (in most cases, all but verbatim) and afterward PRN will provide the clippings to prove it. But a fortnight later the story, the product, and the company are all forgotten.

Most companies need – and want – much more from their public relations than just a little noise: they want public relations to make a tangible difference in awareness, perception, trust, and, most importantly, revenue. They want public relations that will help build their business and reputation in China; will help defend it against all manner of rumors, slip-ups, and crises; and will turn their reputation into a competitive advantage that will secure their market and hold back the multiplying cohort of local competitors.

The steps in this chapter will take you a long way toward creating a highly effective public relations program. Follow the steps in this order, and you are literally halfway to doing so:

- Start by knowing why PR is different in China than it is elsewhere. Chances are that you have had experience with public relations elsewhere, or you are reporting to someone at HQ whose experience is entirely abroad. Much of that knowledge will help you in China, but only if you understand how you need to alter your approaches to adjust to some of the core differences in the market.

- Understand why and how PR is misunderstood in China by your colleagues, customers, competitors and regulators, and comprehend why you need to address that upfront.
- Know all of your publics in China, and be able to prioritize them so you know where to focus your time and resources.
- Place PR in the correct place in a China organization to ensure maximum effectiveness.
- Build a PR team in China, whether it is just one person, a small team and an agency, or a large department.
- Create a China public relations plan that will drive the business forward.
- Avoid the ethical traps that ensnare public relations efforts in China.
- Recruit your most important spokespeople: your China executives.

Addressing misconceptions about PR

A key challenge you will face are the deep misconceptions about public relations that can hamper anyone trying to run a campaign in the PRC. For the reasons noted above, public relations in China has necessarily evolved in response to the unique circumstances of the market, the changes that market is undergoing, and the needs that companies have as a result. The speed of change and the things that make China a singular challenge have created a lot of confusion about what PR is and what it can do.

Not just media relations: The most common misconception is that PR in China is synonymous with media relations or press agentry. While media are traditionally the most influential intermediary and a sizable number of PR agencies in China offer almost nothing other than media relations, PR must encompass a far greater range of audiences and channels. Indeed, a campaign waged to convince Chinese journalists of the greatness of a company and the value of its product will not necessarily burnish a company's brand or improve its business prospects. For that reason, PR must address more than just media, a point we take up below when talking about *publics* and *audiences*.

The "PR girls" problem: In the early days of China's industrialization, factory managers would often bring attractive young women to business meetings. The idea (in its most innocent form) was that the mere presence of these comely young ladies would smooth business dealings between two work units. These young women were called *gong guan xiaojie*, or "public relations girls." As a result, many older Chinese executives have had a hard time taking public relations seriously, an attitude they have often passed on to younger colleagues.

PR as propaganda: Language adds to the confusion over PR's proper role. Common usage in mainland China has turned "publicity" and "propaganda" into synonyms: they are both translations of the word *xianchuan*, which is how PR is commonly described. The problem is that simply using the term makes PR sound like a single-sided, top-down, manipulative, and evil-tinged process. Good PR is none of those things, and this adds to cynicism about the value of public relations.

PR as a part of marketing: Another common misconception stems from the common decision to place PR under marketing or to limit its duties to supporting the "go-to-market" function in a company. PR certainly has a role to play in marketing, *earning* attention, awareness, and trust to complement attention that is paid for (via advertising, point-of-sale, etc.). But because it addresses audiences and issues beyond the customers and the channel, PR cannot be effective if it is limited to marketing function.

PR as "communications": To get away from some of these misconceptions, many managers and public relations professionals in China have taken to calling the craft "communications." This is both too narrow and too broad. It is too broad because corporate functions outside of the scope of PR – such as sales and advertising – are also forms of communications. It is too narrow because a company's PR includes not only what it says, but what it does. Nearly every action and behavior that a company undertakes has a public relations dimension: concept cars are as much about PR as they are about design; the decision to set up a factory in China – and then in what city to set up that factory – is as much a PR effort as it is an operational decision; the legion of companies that made donations to earthquake relief in Sichuan in 2008 did so as a matter of public relations; and when a Chinese company lists its shares on the NYSE or NASDAQ, it is as often about gaining stature as it is about financial need.

Even the most prosaic of company actions serve as unintentional PR assets – or liabilities. Microsoft's decision to offer a different type of warranty on its Surface Pro tablets in China than it does overseas was a tiny decision that turned into a major crisis. Motorola's decision in 2009 to close its local service centers and hand over its warranty work to a contractor was a far larger public relations challenge than it was an operational issue. And Goldman-Sachs's employment of the child of a former Chinese leader in a relatively unimportant role helped frame the way Chinese think about the investment bank and its operations in China. Actions and behaviors have PR value, often beyond mere communications. As long as that is the case, those actions and behaviors must be seen as part of a company's overall public relations effort.

To eliminate misconceptions, it helps to give a clear definition of public relations that is relevant in the China context:

Public relations in China is the sum of actions, behaviors, and communications conducted by an organization with the intent of informing and influencing the groups that have a role in the organization's success.

Know your publics

Armed with an understanding of PR's importance in China and the broader issues that frame a PR effort, we can start building an effective program. That effort necessarily begins with enumerating those groups, or "publics," that can influence the company's prospects in China and how they relate to one another. This might be straightforward elsewhere, but because of China's size, its culture, its politics, and its stage of economic development, a company's publics evolve over time, and frequently shift in role and importance.

Many of your company's publics in China and their relative importance will depend on its industry, its business model, and the state of development of its sector, as well as how government policy affects that sector. Generally speaking, though, a company's publics that must be addressed by PR extend far beyond the media. Typical publics in China include:

Academics: China is one of those places in the world where academic achievement and an academic life is still a matter of prestige, and for that reason experts attached to research and learning institutions are respected voices among audiences in the PRC. Without going too deeply into why (academic achievement was the primary means of social mobility in imperial China), this is likely to remain the case for some time. By academics, we mean not just university professors, but also researchers attached to institutions like the Chinese Academy of Social Sciences (CASS,) the Chinese Academy of Science (CAS,) the National Development and Reform Commission (NDRC,) the People's Bank of China, or the Ministry of Agriculture. Researchers and lecturers are liberally speckled throughout the Chinese government, professional and business associations, quasi-governmental organizations, China's growing raft of non-governmental organizations (NGOs), and even (to a degree) the media.

Activists: One does not usually think about activists as influencers in China because of the way the party responds to political voices outside of government. Nonetheless, China does have a small but important legion of "legal" activists, most of whom are deeply patriotic and often quite shrill about their patriotism. From the masses of online posters that are part of China's 50-Cent Army to the CCTV host who made it a personal campaign to get Starbucks kicked out of the precincts around the Forbidden City, this group operates outside of government control yet serves the government's ends. Its members are the first to see an anti-Chinese conspiracy at the heart of every act by a foreign company. They look and sound like gadflies; but, as Starbucks discovered, they can often be far more threatening and need to be taken seriously.

Celebrities: The simultaneous growth of China's media and economy has created a celebrity culture that vaults singers, athletes, screen stars, and successful entrepreneurs into a limelight once reserved for party leaders. The attention and admiration these people receive are natural magnets for companies seeking to build a brand or promote a product, and many of China's celebrities make far more money from sponsorship and endorsement deals than from their primary professions. But celebrities can be expensive, high-maintenance, and fickle, and China's increasingly cynical consumers understand that few endorsements are much more that quid pro quo deals. Earn the genuine patronage of a group of celebrities, however, (or even just keep them away from the competition) and you have marketing gold.

Consumers: This is fairly self-explanatory. If you sell products or services for which consumers are the end user, they are your market, and everything public relations does in communicating to consumers is in some way a sales-support function. Yet even if they are not your direct customers, their behaviors and attitudes influence your actual customers and your regulators. As such, every company should consider the role that consumers play in their PR.

Customers: Although some companies confuse "customers" and "consumers," they are usually not the same. Most businesses – even those producing consumer goods – do not sell directly to consumers, but to intermediaries like distributors and retailers. Those buying directly from a company are customers, while "consumers" are the final, end users of a product or service. Each group needs to be addressed appropriately, but customers remain the top public in China: the most important work that PR can do is to provide direct support to sales. An essential goal of PR should be to reduce the salesperson's role to taking orders and taking the customer to lunch.

Distributors and retailers: Regardless of who the customer and the ultimate consumer may be, a core public for most companies is the sales channel, the total chain of intermediaries that form a link between the company and the ultimate consumer of its product. In industries with long sales channels, a key part of PR is not only supporting a company's team in selling product, but also helping customers sell the product onward down the channel to their customers, even when that product changes form in the process or becomes a component of another, larger product. Companies that will rarely sell a product to a consumer – think Boeing, Airbus, Qualcomm, NVIDIA, and Intel – still conduct consumer PR in China to help their customers sell their products by establishing their value as an ingredient brand.

Employees: The single most overlooked audience in China is the internal audience: employees and their families. While most companies understand the value of sustaining the morale of employees by keeping them informed, that function is often relegated to human resources (HR) departments, which in China are rarely capable of planning or conducting a program designed to inform, inspire, and activate employees as informal spokespeople. Before the advent of social media, this was a wasted opportunity. Today, nearly all Chinese employees of a modern urban company have some form of social media, and most have several. For this reason, in many companies employees are more important intermediaries than even the media.

General interest media: General interest media include newspapers, news magazines, most radio stations, and the general interest channels of China's broadcasters, such as CCTV Channel 1, Oriental Television, Guangdong TV 1, and Beijing TV 1. These media have a wide footprint, are able to influence a large swathe of the population, and are often at the forefront of investigative crusades aimed at foreign companies. It is common in China for bloggers, online publications, and online video sites to "borrow" content from these outlets, multiplying the effect of particularly salacious stories.

Industry analysts: A relatively new public in China is formed from the growing ranks of industry analysts. Initially these were concentrated in Hong Kong and focused on the telecommunications and technology industries, but over the years the large global analyst houses have moved onshore, and the range of industries has diversified. Industry analysts rarely move markets by themselves, but they are increasingly used as sources of quotes and insights by the media and other companies, and therefore are growing in importance as influencers.

Key opinion leaders: These are individuals, probably members of one or more of the other groups, who by dint of their personal credibility and renown are extraordinarily important as influencers. With the growth of social media, they have become a critical part of any successful program in China. Gaining and sustaining the support of key influencers is difficult, but it can be extremely rewarding.

Lifestyle media: As China's people become more prosperous, they have begun to look for ways to experience life in a manner different from their parents or even their peers. Lifestyle media are one of the largest drivers of the breakdown of China's mass market, and lie at the nexus of geographically dispersed communities ranging from car enthusiasts to cosplay fans to citizens concerned about China's environment. These media do more than just report the news – they are often tastemakers and trendsetters in their own right.

Local community: Any company with a physical facility in China needs to be concerned about relationships with the local community. This is especially the case for companies with manufacturing or processing facilities located in or near villages or major population centers. As China's petroleum giants have discovered, even the explicit support of the central government is insufficient to keep local communities from causing tremendous trouble when there is an incident or even the threat of one. If a state-owned enterprise has to forge ties with the local citizenry, doing so is doubly incumbent on a foreign company.

Local authorities: A part of any local community outreach begins with the local authorities of a county, village, township, or city. The list of key entities runs from the offices of the mayor and/or Party secretary (the latter of course being the more powerful of the two) to the local tax office, the bureau of industry and commerce, the public security bureau, and a range of other local organizations that have immediate – or potential – interest in a company's business in a given location. (This public includes not only the officials themselves, but also their staff, many of whom wield the true power. Do not be fooled by the relatively low level of the officials involved and their potential remoteness from Beijing and even from a provincial capital: local officials can be a company's greatest allies or most implacable foes. Keeping them informed and engaged and sustaining their support is essential for success, and the stakes rise with the level of investment in a given locality.)

Local media: Most PR efforts focus on national and provincial media, ignoring the smaller media outlets in the local communities around their facilities. Yet these organizations are among the most critical – they are more likely to provide aid and support in return for access, and can be essential in winning over the local community and authorities; they can also prove a key locus of support in a crisis.

National government entities: When most people think of the Chinese government, they think about the national authorities based in Beijing. As we will discuss in Chapter 2, for most foreign companies, the national government is often the second most important public a company faces after customers, and during market entry and times of great change the government can be the single most important public of all.

National media: China has dozens of media outlets whose circulation or footprint reaches far beyond a single locality or province. Usually, these are of the highest quality, have the highest visibility, and are the most influential among China's media. Unsurprisingly, this is the public with which PR teams concern themselves the most. More about them is discussed in Chapter 3.

Online personalities: The growth of the internet, the rigid nature of programming on television, and the stifling environments in most Chinese media outlets have driven some of China's most interesting personalities to build an identity online, outside of the mainstream media. The growing rejection of mainstream media by Chinese born after 1980 has enabled the rise of an entire class of experts, commentators, and talking heads to come to prominence. Some of China's most popular chefs, technologists, and self-help gurus are not formally employed by any media, choosing instead to create their own mini-empires from social media, websites, columns, guest appearances, book publishing, e-commerce, and sponsorships. Even the most prosaic fields have their experts and personalities, and after a few spectacular failures, the majority have learned how to take corporate coin while maintaining their credibility with their fans, walking the line between selling themselves and selling out.

Prospective employees: Anyone who has engaged in a talent search in China for something more complex than a no-skill, entry-level position will confirm that while China is rich in candidates, it is still relatively poor in talent. For that reason, a key public is the universe of prospective employees that a company would like to hire. These may be engineers in graduate school or a group of top salespeople working in fast-moving consumer goods. Most HR departments are tasked with reaching out to prospective employees but are ill-equipped to do so.

Prosumers: Somewhere between consumers and the channel lie a group of self-made experts in your industry, best known as prosumers. In China, this particular breed of self-appointed specialist has neither a formal position nor a soapbox, and may be a miniature version of an online personality – albeit, with somewhat more modest followings. Prosumers are most often associated with consumer electronics, and specifically hardcore gamers, photography enthusiasts, and collectors, but are not limited to these fields. Even companies like Boeing and Airbus have several classes of prosumers, ranging from very frequent flyers to plane-spotters. These are people with tremendous knowledge, a great deal of respect from peers, and an ability to turn that enthusiasm into a wider following.

Provincial government entities: Located on the scale between the national government and local government, local provincial entities tend to get involved with enterprises at three different times: (1) at the beginning when approvals are sought; (2) if the national government takes an interest in the enterprise; and (3) when there is a crisis. Provincial support can be a powerful advantage when seeking help in Beijing and can be the nexus of great challenges in a crisis.

Think-tanks: Of growing importance in China is a class of semi-autonomous institutes and organizations that spend their time focused on a single area or a few areas of policy. These organizations have a growing status, particularly in Beijing but also in provincial capitals and first-tier cities, because the formulation of policy and the affects of policy are becoming much more complex than many regulators are capable of addressing. Think-tanks take on the roles of analysts and recommenders in the process, and are therefore becoming more important.

Your publics and your success

In the course of your planning and PR activities, each of these publics needs to be addressed. Many PR teams, especially smaller ones, dissipate their efforts trying to respond to all of them at once. In an ideal world, we would all have skilled teams with adequate resources assigned to all of our publics. The reality is that this is almost never the case. For that reason, it is necessary to conduct some triage: not all are equally important, so you will need to prioritize publics based on the degree to which they can drive – or block – your success. The best way to do this is to get the entire China leadership team into a conference room for an hour and conduct an audience analysis.

Start by asking the team about all of the things that serve as a roadblock to success, and write them down on a white board or a sheet of paper enough for all to see. Focus on the outside of the company, but if there are significant internal issues that come up, include those as well. Then create a separate, but parallel list of all of the factors that are driving the company to reach its goals in China. By a show of hands, have everyone vote on which issues they think are the most pressing.

Then pass around your list of publics. Work through them one by one. Ask which of them most directly affect the company's success – this part should be easy. The resulting list will show you your target audiences. Next, ask the team to prioritize those audiences. That will give you your list of priorities, in order. On a clean board or a sheet of white paper, list those publics down the center in a column.

Then ask people which publics – either on the sheet or not listed – are best positioned to influence your audiences. List those out, on either side of the audiences. These are your key influencers. Draw a line from each influencer group to the audience they influence. Finally, ask the team to prioritize the 2–3 most important key influencers for each of your target audiences. What you will wind up with at the end of this is a very clear prioritization. Your audiences are your first priority, and your leading influencers for each group are your second priority. When you start planning your PR program, you will focus on these groups.

"What about the other audiences?" you ask. There is no simple answer for that. Each needs to be addressed, but what you will find is that some can be addressed indirectly (for example, prosumers can often be addressed through channel marketing programs), others can be addressed on a contingency basis (such as local communities), and still others can be handled primarily by other functions in the company, requiring you only to provide support (this is often how employees are addressed, via the HR function).

In the case of those you cannot address right away, come back to them once you have your plan in place, and as you execute your plan look for ways to include these audiences. The following is a great example of this: A mobile device manufacturer made a habit of inviting local officials from the cities in which they had factories to all major product launches held in China, where they treated them like VIPs. The officials ate it up and felt like they were part of the team. The company also made a point of including them in its press release distribution lists, allowing them bragging rights in meetings in Beijing or with other officials. This may sound trivial, but it is through goodwill gestures like this that genuine progress is made.

A few more thoughts about addressing your audiences: First, do not get into the habit of having a different set of messages for each audience. Not only might different groups compare notes, you will often have people who are members of more than one audience. Almost everyone you work with is, for example, a consumer, so saying one thing to consumers and another to government officials will quickly get you into trouble. The same goes for audiences outside of China. While there was once a time when what you said to media inside of China rarely got past the language barrier, today many wire services (Bloomberg being chief among them) make a habit of searching the local media for tidbits on companies and running them over their newswire. The same happens in reverse. So what you say in Beijing does not stay in Beijing. Consistency in China and about China is essential to your credibility.

Second, be as transparent as you can without endangering proprietary information or placing yourself in violation of the law. Transparency not only ensures that you are consistent; it also makes it easier to address audiences that you may not have the resources to work with directly. Finally, the best way to start addressing your audiences is often not directly but through your highest priority influencers (it will take you some time to cultivate the best influencers, so it is best to start immediately). There are some good reasons for this strategy: influencers can often provide important insights about your target audience in advance of reaching out directly; and it is always easier to approach your target audiences directly (and with credibility) when they have already heard about you from third parties. Furthermore, the primary communications goal of public relations is to ensure that people are hearing good things about the company, its brand, and its products from credible third parties far more than from the company itself.

Organizing public relations

An important question that bedevils both general management and public relations professionals is the matter of where the PR team belongs in the organization. To whom should they report? Who do they advise? And what is their primary function within the organization? These questions have to be asked even before you start hiring a PR team.

There is no perfect answer to this: every organization faces unique challenges in China that will determine the PR team's most important roles and where it sits. If the company's overwhelming challenge is demand generation, PR will likely fit under marketing. If the company is a production facility that ships all of its products overseas or it supervises a series of joint ventures, PR may need to report to operations.

In most companies in China, public relations serves neither purely a corporate/operations function nor strictly a marketing/marcoms function, but an admixture of both. Even those public relations departments most focused on marketing are called upon to provide support in a crisis, and the most "corporate" public relations teams will concern themselves with brand and product marketing to some degree. When making the decision of who will oversee the public relations effort, it is essential to understand the full scope of what PR may be called upon to do.

The first step in that process is assessing a company's audiences, as we have done above. The second step is to consider the kinds of challenges that public relations might be called upon to support in China. In addition to supporting marketing campaigns, public relations also supports the following:

Sales: particularly in business-to-business companies, through support of activities at trade shows and by engaging with and generating coverage in trade media.

Human resources: often by taking on internal communications activities and, in many industries, conducting external public relations work that supports recruitment and retention.

Legal: particularly when a company is planning or is engaged in legal action in China, to help build public and government support for a specific case or principle (a critical part of the legal effort, especially in a country where the courts rule based on political expediency as often as they do on the law itself).

Government relations: often by taking charge of the government relations portfolio, but at the very least by ensuring that messages delivered to the government are consistent with those being delivered to other audiences.

Community relations: by conducting activities designed to demonstrate the positive role a company plays in its local community, a function of acute importance for manufacturing, energy, and processing industries where mishaps that affect the public are a latent risk.

Operations: by preparing for potential crises and for conducting proactive programs designed to cast the company as a whole in the best possible light among local government, partners, suppliers, and the industry in China.

Finance: at the very least by ensuring that executives do not communicate undisclosed material information about the company, and that all communications take into account shareholder interests and concerns.

Customer service: by working to ensure that appropriate channels for customer concerns and complaints are adequately addressed, and by ensuring repair, recall, and return information is made quickly available during a customer service crisis.

Procurement: by making the company appear to be a desirable customer, thus helping to improve the terms of business with local suppliers.

Business development: by laying the groundwork to enable the company to extend into other provinces, other cities, or other lines of business in China.

The complexity of these varying functions and the time that they can take away from the marketing effort have caused many larger companies to split the public relations function, with one public relations executive or team designated to handle marketing communications (in support of the sales and go-to-market effort), and another executive or team charged with supporting all of the other corporate functions.

The marketing communications–corporate communications split has proven effective for handling the tactical work, but too many companies make the mistake of failing to ensure adequate coordination between the two teams. At best, this can lead to turf battles that cause friction and distraction. At worst, it can mean that each team figures that an issue is a problem for the other, and so the problem does not get addressed in a timely fashion. Coordination is essential: the best route to that is to ensure that both teams report to the same executive, whether this is someone outside the team, or the senior of the two team leaders.

Organizing around publics

Not all companies would have the full scope of concerns outlined above, particularly in the early stages. For some companies the issues are even broader. But public relations must be organized to be able to provide support across all corporate functions when their work and concerns touch on the company's publics. It may not seem necessary now, but over time it will be, and usually before you expect it.

Initially, a single individual would take charge of working with the full range of publics – media, analysts, customers, the channel, government, investors, and the community. This should be handled with the assistance of an agency team able to serve as an on-demand resource to help the PR manager adjust to the demands on his or her time.

Agencies can be expensive, however, and convenience and economics dictate that at some point you will want to expand the internal team. When doing so, the best approach is to hire people who are suited to working with a specific public or set of publics. Your second hire should be someone able to support your government and community relations, and then assist with media relations as they are able. After that, hire staff based on the anticipated level of activity with a given group. This ensures that each new resource will be focused on the audience with the most pressing need.

Once fully grown, the public relations department should thus have a staff that includes:

- A go-to-market media relations team focused on supporting marketing campaigns, aimed at consumers, customers, the channel, prosumers, and the media that address them all.

- A corporate media relations team focused on business media, financial media, industry analysts, and global media interested less in your products and more on your business as a whole.
- A public affairs team focused on supporting the company executives in their outreach to regulators at the national, provincial, and local levels, to the embassy of the country where the company is based, and to the local community at large.
- If your company in China is either listed on one of the regional exchanges or is a regionally listed subsidiary of an overseas firm, it will also be necessary to have a financial communications team able to respond to basic inquiries from shareholders (both individuals and institutions), investment advisors, financial analysts, and even regulators.

The digital question

The newness of social media and the lack of clarity on how to deal with it have compelled many companies to relegate digital communications and social media to a separate department. While companies are getting to know digital, there is validity to this approach. But as companies become familiar with these new media, they quickly discover that they are not distinct publics, but extremely interactive channels by which to reach their most important audiences. Having separate "digital" and "traditional" teams all addressing the same audiences is a prescription for confusion, turf battles, and lost opportunities.

The best approach is to designate a small digital team to understand emerging social media, develop capabilities and practices for addressing them, and then disseminate that information to the audience-focused teams. The digital team also serves as a point of coordination, ensuring that the company's online "personality" does not get lost in a jumble of unrelated content. In this way, social media, like online publications, television, radio, and print before them, become an effective tool for appropriately reaching all audiences.

Consultants and social media specialists will try to convince you to separate out "digital" or "social media" from your other marketing or PR functions in China. Resist that: it serves only those who seek to build their own independent empire and does not serve the interests of the company as a whole. Hiving off social media only serves to isolate a critical set of capabilities from the company as a whole, unnecessarily complicating coordination and communications.

Leadership is key

There is no right or wrong answer about how to structure a PR team in China. I have worked with very large companies with a single individual running PR with the help of an outside agency; and Apple, for its part, uses only internal teams for its China PR. Strong leadership, though, is essential. With a variety of publics to address, the external relations effort must be led by a single individual overseeing a combined communications function.

That individual might be the chief marketing officer, the head of operations, or, in larger companies, a "chief communications officer," which is a sort of super-PR manager. Whichever way, one person needs to ensure that teams are coordinated, do not overlap or duplicate effort, and deliver consistent messages across the entire scope of publics. The latter is essential: nothing ruins a company's credibility more quickly than when, for example, government officials are told one thing, and newspapers are told another. Regulators tend to get upset when they discover in the morning news that you have lied to them.

Experience is proof: the companies that recruit the most capable public relations managers are the ones whose PR teams become a competitive advantage. Given the challenges you face in China, you cannot afford anything less.

Recruiting the team

Now that you have organized the China public relations function, it is time for your most daunting challenge: recruiting the PR team (even if, at first, it is only a team of one). This is no small issue: next to the PR budget, the challenge of recruiting the first PR person for the company is the single factor that slows the timely creation of a PR function. I have known a few China general managers who, when faced with the requirement from HQ to recruit for a PR function, balk: "Why," they ask, "do I need to spend the time and money to find a PR person in the first place?" To a cost- and time-conscious executive, it can be tempting to follow the advice of entrepreneur Jason Calcanis, who suggested that every chief executive officer (CEO) should do his own PR.

That urge does not last long: while such an approach may make sense for a one-person, bootstrapped operation with a tight budget, it is pound-foolish for companies that are large, will grow quickly, or are the local presence of a large global organization. For such companies, the time demands placed on a local chief executive quickly makes having the general manager or regional CEO directly overseeing the PR function totally impracticable. Sales, marketing, and operations draw time and attention away from PR, just as the business begins to grow and journalists, analysts, the government, and local community leaders start calling in earnest. At that point, the question becomes "how do I find someone to handle this stuff right now?"

If you wait until you really need a PR person, you are already late. Hire your first China PR person, the prospective team leader mentioned above, just as soon as you can – start the search immediately. Qualified, experienced, and competent corporate PR people are surprisingly hard to come by, and finding one that will fit into your corporate culture makes the search infinitely more challenging. For that reason, searches for an individual that you can trust to be your PR lead can take anywhere from two to six months, even with the help of a good headhunter, especially when your best candidate is likely to already have a job.

If you find yourself in immediate need of PR help, avoid the temptation to hire the first moderately presentable candidate who comes through the door. This is an important role, and you are strongly advised not to rush the decision of who to hire. In the meantime, a good short-term fix is to hire an agency that will either assemble a team to act as a virtual PR department, or might even be able to second a competent and sharp PR person to you until you have identified the right candidate. Quite a few companies have even identified the ideal candidate through this process. The agency will not only help you define the short-term challenges, they should also be able to assemble a PR plan to use as a starting point, come up with a job description, and even help you vet candidates.

Skills and qualities of the China PR manager

There are a range of capabilities and skills to look for in any good manager, but for someone who is going to lead a public relations effort, a few traits stick out. Experience is important. For someone who is going to lead the PR function of a small organization, 3–5 years' experience should be sufficient. For the leader of a mid-sized company with a modest amount of outside work, you should look for 7–8 years' experience. And to lead the local communications for an NYSE- or NASDAQ-listed firm, you will want a candidate with a decade or more experience. You will not always be able to find someone with experience in your industry, but you will want someone who has the skills and background to understand your business. Hiring a PR manager for an innovative industrial company and a market made up of engineering firms, you probably should not be looking at a candidate who has spent a career selling luxury consumer baubles. While some experience transfers, you are going to spend far too much time getting the person up to speed.

Next to experience, language skills are critical. If your firm is international, you will want someone who can communicate in the language of the home country and who can speak fluent, native-level Chinese. Don't bother hiring someone who cannot read and write (as well as speak) Chinese at university level: if they cannot read a newspaper and catch linguistic nuances, they cannot be your candidate. Ideally, you want someone who can read, write, and speak both languages with fluency and comfort.

You want someone with a personality that is strong enough to be able to offer opinions that may run counter to those of other managers, and to do so with conviction. A PR manager who cannot say "no" to his or her colleagues and boss will disappoint in the long run, and in a crisis situation will be worse than useless. Also, keep in mind that public relations as a profession in China is around 70% female. If you run an organization with a strong "guy" culture, make sure you hire someone who will fit into that culture rather than be offended by it. This does not, however, excuse your team from being gentlemen.

You will naturally want someone with strong media relations skills and good familiarity with the way government works. Experience in – or working with – an agency is a plus, because effectively managing an agency means walking that often narrow middle ground between letting the agency run you and riding gratuitously roughshod over an agency just to "show 'em who is the boss." The less experience the person has with agencies, the more likely they are to have a problematic agency relationship and impair the effectiveness of the PR effort.

You want someone who has the ability to mentor others. Even if your PR department never grows beyond a single person, the PR function involves constant coaching of colleagues and company leaders. The ability to impart skills and techniques to others is an essential part of the PR manager's toolkit.

Finally, you want something that few people talk about: integrity. Almost every other skill I have listed above can be taught or communicated, but integrity must be an innate part of the character of the individual. When you hire a PR manager, you are selecting an individual in whom you are going to entrust the company's reputation with outside audiences. You cannot afford to put that in the hands of someone who will always place his or her own interests above "doing the right thing."

Unfortunately, integrity is not something you can demonstrate on a résumé or a LinkedIn profile, and it is something that is extraordinarily difficult to find in China. The ugly, politically incorrect truth is that over the past 70 years China has produced three generations of people who have learned to get by in the worst of times by taking care of Number One. There are good people out there, but you need to look for them, and you should not take people at face value.

There are different ways to test for integrity – use different interviewers, ask situation-specific questions, and the like. My favorite approach is the core-competency interview. A quick check online will introduce you to the technique. It is well worth the hour or two invested to craft a relevant core-competency interview process; you can even check with a recruiting firm if they can provide some assistance. In the long-term it will be well worth the investment.

Finally, if you can afford to do so, once you have a finalist, put them in front of as many of your colleagues – and your trusted advisors – as you can. Chances are good that they will see things (both positive and negative) that you will not, and you need to make sure that this person can get along with the folks that you rely on every day.

Where to find a China PR manager

Once you know what you are looking for, there comes the brutal challenge of actually finding one or more viable candidates. As noted above, your PR agency might be of help, simply because they, too, are probably on the constant lookout for candidates and may have someone a little too senior for an agency, who would work out well for you. Next, ask around among people you can trust who have an idea of the kinds of challenges you will face as a company. You would be surprised how many companies find their PR people through their social and professional circles. Try not to hire someone recommended by a customer, a competitor, or a supplier: what you might be doing is hiring a spy, so use extreme caution when you reach out to people who have an interest in knowing what happens inside your business.

Failing the above, roll up your sleeves and start looking online. LinkedIn has over five million members in China, and at the time of writing the vast majority had profiles in English. There are local competitors to the LinkedIn service, but what makes LinkedIn such an effective place to go looking for PR people is that the people using the service tend to have foreign language skills and be internationally minded, two key qualifications for a PR manager. There are also a huge number of PR people on LinkedIn, so you will have an opportunity to scan through a lot of profiles to get an idea of who is out there.

If that does not work out for you, or if you simply don't have the time to shuffle though thousands of profiles, you are left with having to go to a headhunter. Most of the major global recruitment firms have significant operations in China, but you want to look for one that has a specialization in marketing and public relations people. The best recruiting firms tend to have consultants who map out entire fields of specialization and know who is out there – they can usually locate a handful of worthy clients in the space of a few weeks. This is an expensive option, but if you have other things to do and you are not familiar with the territory, companies like Hudson or Spencer-Stuart may be the best way to go.

The one thing you should not do for a position like this is place ads with online job sites – unless you are ready to be buried in a pile of résumés of indeterminate veracity in the space of a few days. If you do not have time to wade through LinkedIn, this is not the approach for you. But if you have plenty of time, less money, and LinkedIn is not working for you, place your ads, put on a pot of coffee, and get down to the business of sifting through replies.

The onboarding process

Once you have found the right candidate, and before you start planning your public relations program, invest the time to properly onboard the candidate. Having somebody helping the company understand its publics and then communicate to them when the individual in question has only a superficial understanding of your business is asking for a middling outcome. At the very least, make sure that the new PR manager not only meets his or her colleagues, but spends a day shadowing each one to learn what they do and how they do it. If your company has a PR team elsewhere in the world – for example, at HQ or a large subsidiary, or even that local agency you hired for the interim – make sure the new recruit gets as much face time (virtual or real) with them as possible. This will allow your new team member to absorb the way things are done in the company now, and allow them the opportunity to get up to speed.

If you have hired an agency, have them provide a complete briefing to the new hire, explaining what was has been done to date; also have the agency provide a summary of work in progress, contacts made, and a complete list of media, analysts, and officials.

This orientation process should take about a week to 10 days, adding more for international travel to HQ (if applicable). Once orientation is complete, the first order of business is to have the PR manager reach out personally to all of the media, analysts, and government entities with which the organization has had interaction to introduce himself/herself as the new point of contact. Particularly in the case of government entities, the CEO or General Manager should make the introductions in person, and should be clear as to the role the individual will play going forward.

Once this has been done, it is time to start planning the work itself. Have the PR manager spend 2–3 days framing a public relations plan that reflects your business plans for the coming year.

PR plans in China

Responsive PR is good as far as it goes, but the truth is that responsive PR hands the initiative to your rivals. PR in China cannot be used only as a shield: if you are a market leader, rivals will seize the PR initiative, spreading rumors that will erode and eventually destroy your reputation. If you are not a market leader, you will be ignored. For that reason, taking the initiative in public relations should be your first goal, and you will need to plan in order to do that.

The process of planning a public relations campaign in China is about 90% the same as it is elsewhere, so we will focus here only on what is either different or needs extra emphasis. For now, let's focus on what you need to know to survive that process and come up with an effective PR plan for China.

Be forewarned: planning PR in China can be frustrating. By the time you have done your research, learned the targets for the coming year, brainstormed some superb ideas, framed everything into a plan and gained the approval of leadership, the plan may well be obsolete. Business priorities change, crises happen, and the sheer speed of change in China conspires to prove the old Yiddish adage that "man plans, God laughs."

What makes the process even more challenging is that by the time you sit down to write your first PR plan the pressure from above to just "get on with it" will be tremendous: journalists will be calling; there will be press releases to write, translate, and distribute; a senior executive wants to do a photo-op in a new factory, there is a store-opening to prepare, and there is negative buzz on Weixin. In an ideal world, you would have the time to plan before doing. Conditions are rarely ideal in China, and most public relations teams hit the ground running hard just to catch up.

For this reason, your initial planning will have to take place alongside execution. The downside is that this will make your initial activity feel like so much aimless wheel-spinning, gratifying initially but lacking the promise of sustained momentum. Take heart: the advantages of planning-as-you-go, at least for the first plan, outweigh the downsides. Simply capturing initial ad-hoc opportunities serves as a test for the kinds of tactics and messaging that work, and will teach you a lot about what won't work. *Not* immediately sitting down and conducting public relations work (especially, as noted above, if the company is behind the curve in that respect) would be worse for the company – and for the PR function – than addressing immediate challenges and opportunities without a plan. And finally, some initial work internally and with external publics will take a lot of the guesswork out of the planning process.

As you start the process, keep a laser focus on the broader business objective. This can be a challenge. You will be sorely tempted to set out loose objectives like "growing awareness" or more parochial PR objectives like "achieve a target of 1 million characters written about the company per quarter." Resist. While these objectives have the advantage of being clear, measurable, and achievable (as all good objectives should be), they are not meaningful in a business sense. Even if you cannot tie PR efforts directly to sales (and a growing number of companies can), set objectives that get closer to the business. Something simple like "gain favorable coverage in China's top ten lifestyle magazines," or "increase unprompted awareness of our brand among Shanghai men by 50%" are better, but you should try to set objectives like "increase traffic to our site by 25% while doubling conversion rates," or "drive a 15% increase in off-season retail sell-through." Regardless of what you decide, remember that getting return on investment (ROI) out of public relations in China demands objectives that, if achieved, will *prima facie* move the business a considerable distance toward its overall objectives in China.

This focus on business objectives will translate to a focus on PR efforts. While it may not seem so at first, the opportunities you will have to engage with publics in China are numerous. Even companies in the most prosaic of industries find themselves facing dozens of media, a handful of engaged analysts and opinion leaders, half a dozen major trade shows a year, several thousand people in the business on social media, and a corps of interested government officials, and for most industries those groups are far larger. Opportunities will multiply quickly, and you will soon find yourself overwhelmed by interesting speaking engagements, interview requests, trade show invitations, and online conversations. Creating and sticking to a plan that is driven by business objectives should never be so rigid that you ignore genuinely worthy ad hoc opportunities. What it will do is impose a filter that will cull all but those that will make a genuine difference to the enterprise. A good China PR plan is, therefore, a systematic program of interaction with your publics designed to help the company achieve its China business objectives within the time, resources, and budgets allotted.

Finally, as you go about planning for public relations in China, there are several critical rules that you should keep in mind to ensure that your planning will be a success:

1. **Don't make planning a fetish:** It is too easy in China to get wrapped up in the planning process – doing research, brainstorming ideas, and developing better and better versions of the plan. There will always be more to learn and unknowns to address; it feels safer and more comforting to plan than it does to take the risk of proactive public relations. Get over it: give yourself a hard deadline to come up with a final plan, obtain input from your team and leadership, and make a start. If it takes you more than a week to develop a six-month plan, you are overthinking the process.

2. **Do not do full-year or multi-year plans:** China's complexity and the speed with which the market moves and competitors respond make attempting to plan for a full year – or more – unrealistic. Instead, approach planning as a rolling process whereby you are planning three to six months ahead on an ongoing basis. This does not mean that you cannot build a rough framework for the plan going forward. What it does mean is that your detailed plans should never run more than six months ahead, or less than three months ahead. Not only will following this approach make planning faster and easier, it will make it more realistic, and it will enable you to ensure that your plans stay apace with the market.

3. **Seek guidance, but do not wait for it:** As outlined above, the best China public relations builds on local business and marketing plans and mesh with plans in other parts of the world. Ideally, that information is available to you in a timely fashion and in a form that you can use. Despite everyone's best intentions, this may not always be the case. Business and marketing

planning processes for China are fraught due to a range of factors beyond the control of you or your colleagues. Reach out for guidance from colleagues in other functions and based in other regions, explain that you have a strict deadline (give them a week to 10 days), and don't wait: write the plan. At the very least, you will have thought through the challenges and opportunities, built a plan, and have insights to share. What is more, simply sharing a complete plan will compel colleagues to respond, and may even end up driving their thinking.

4. **Avoid the temptation to simply replicate the global PR plan in China:** While global plans offer a trove of ideas that can serve as inspiration, local public relations must be driven primarily by local business objectives, guided by market perception and the local competitive environment. Only after those considerations are taken into account should the global plan be allowed to frame the PR effort. In many companies it will be politically impossible to disregard the global plan entirely, and it usually makes sense to create a China plan that integrates with the global plan without simply localizing it. Make sure that you broach this early with the global team, and then work with local leadership to engage them in the process. Addressing the local-versus-global split early in the planning process will lay the groundwork for more harmony later.

With the completion of this chapter, you are now ready to plunge into planning an effective public relations program for China. Next, we will dive into what is probably your most important audience: the government.

Case study: Intel

Intel has been operating in the PRC since the late 1980s, when it opened a representative office to help facilitate the sales of its microprocessors to Chinese computer manufacturers. In its 30-year quest to expand its business in China, it faced regular, perplexing obstacles, despite offering a product that was essential to the development of the Chinese computer industry and, indeed, to the Chinese economy as a whole.

Early in its time in China, Intel's leadership took the visionary step of appointing Jim Jarrett to lead their China efforts. In addition to other strengths, Jarrett, an experienced government relations executive, understood that Intel's success in China would demand much more than superior products: it would demand broad support from a range of publics in China, including the government, Intel customers, academia, and the media. Early in his tenure in the PRC Jarrett appointed a Chinese counterpart, Michael Jong, to work directly with him in the effort to win over those audiences.

The two men spent a substantial amount of time in the late 1990s working directly with key audiences, but discovered early on that the key to their success would be a PR team that reported directly to the two of them. The men recruited a group of locally born executives, some with overseas educations, whose focus was on planning and overseeing the PR effort. Dividing their team among audiences, Jarrett and Jong gave each executive a substantial amount of freedom in crafting their programs, but demanded coordination and open discussion. Planning happened as a group, even when execution happened in silos.

This specialized but integrated organization paid off when the company faced significant crises. In late 2003, the Chinese government all but outlawed a critical component of Intel's chipset, threatening to throw the company and the computer industry as a whole into chaos. The initial reaction was frustration, and suggestions about how to respond were framed as such. But the PR team, with senior level access, was able to provide the counsel to direct a more constructive approach. The team was able to respond immediately, working with a range of partners and internal teams to put together a coordinated response. Within weeks, the edict was lifted, and what could have been a disaster left Intel with even more solid relations with its partners, and demonstrated to the government that Intel was an indelible part of China's computer industry.

Today, Intel has an advanced wafer fabrication plant, three major manufacturing facilities, research and development (R&D) centers, and sales offices across China. Beyond simply launching a half-dozen generations of Intel processors, Intel's China PR team proved that because of its integration into the wider company decision-making process, that team had become a competitive advantage for the chipmaker in its most important market.

chapter 2

Public Relations and the Chinese Government

China's government: the audience that never leaves

When the World Bank rates the relative ease of setting up and operating a business in 189 countries in the world, China ranks an embarrassing 90th (http://data.worldbank.org/indicator/IC.BUS. EASE.XQ). The primary reasons for this are found in the policy, regulatory, and administrative roadblocks that the government has strewn on the business playing field. These are occasionally fixed barriers, but more often they are obstacles that crop up almost at random and regularly rewrite the business equation in China.

Obtaining the right to operate a business in China under the best circumstances involves a long and frustrating journey through the bureaucratic bowels of a half-dozen bureaus and ministries. The worst scenario involves a long, costly campaign to gain an exemption from rules, regulations, policy concerns and general hesitation that frustrates businesses that are not specifically permitted under Chinese law, that are new, or that operate in and around "sensitive" sectors.

There is more at work in this process than the cussed self-importance of the apparatchik. The logic behind making companies really work for a business license is that once you have been through a hero's journey just to obtain the right to run a business, you will do everything in your power as a company to avoid endangering that right. And that right is in constant peril. The government at every level and across dozens of bureaucratic silos has the authority and the wherewithal to harass, impede, and even shut down a company on the shakiest legal grounds. If there is a single word to describe the right to do business in China, it is *conditional* – hard to obtain, easy to lose, and under constant review.

Business walks on a tightrope because of Deng Xiaoping. When the doors were opened to allow foreign businesses to come to China, it was not because of Deng's idealistic belief in Western liberal economic principles. It was, rather, born of a practical desire to help China build its industries, accompanied by the hard-nosed realization that the approaches that China had used both before and after the revolution had failed. Deng's goal was to capture the benefits of foreign participation in the Chinese economy (fresh capital, technology, know-how, global market access, and rapid development) without having to endure the downsides (foreign domination of the economy, massive capital outflows, and a permanent role as the sweatshop of global business). Deng's vision was to help China's industries and (especially state-owned) enterprises "stand up" to the point where they could become global competitors.

There were three implicit parts of that policy. First, foreign enterprises were to be allowed into the Chinese economy only as far – and as long – as necessary in order for them to support key development priorities. Second, foreign enterprises were to be excluded from participation in any industry that might place at risk the Party's ability to remain in power, that placed national security at risk, or that placed key economic or political choke points under foreign control. Finally, once local companies had developed to the point where foreign enterprises were no longer necessary, or indeed began inhibiting the development of local enterprises, the foreign enterprises were to be squeezed out of the market by the most practicable means. Even in the face of China's commitments as part of its accession to and membership in the WTO, that policy has not substantively changed.

In short, the business of China is NOT business: all commercial activity must first serve the broader interests of the Party and the nation – or it must credibly be seen to do so. A company's right to operate in China without interference is conditioned on the degree to which that company is seen as a valuable, essential and inextricable part of China's economic fabric and crucial to the attainment of the nation's evolving economic and political goals.

For this reason, the government will always be among your top three publics, and may often be the most important audience you address. All public relations in China must be conducted with the government in mind, and often with the government as the focus, helping the company earn and retain the right to operate in China in moments of crisis and political change as well as periods of stability.

The key function of a public relations team vis-a-vis the government in China is to help the organization and its leaders in the following ways: understand how party doctrine, government policy, the regulatory environment and administrative whim affect the business; identify immediate and potential challenges; understand which are immutable and which are changeable; and understand how the organization needs to behave and communicate as a result.

The decline of government relations as a business tool

"Government relations" is often used in China as a catch-all term to describe the outreach effort that a company makes to both party and government organs at all levels, and the activity that surrounds that outreach. More accurately, the term refers to the direct interaction with government agencies and officials. At first blush, it may seem like this direct interaction is all that is necessary, and a belief persists that as long as one meets the right officials and says the right things, no further effort is required.

At one time in the past, this may have been sufficient. Government relations was the core effort because reaching out to the government even at the most senior levels was a straightforward process. It was possible for foreign companies to meet with senior government ministers, and often even more senior officials. Access of this nature was granted because the government had not yet fully developed a set of rules and policies to govern the most prosaic aspects of government oversight of businesses that were not directly subordinate to a given ministry. Simply to gain a business license it was necessary to arrange a meeting with a senior personage, who, if all went well, would direct the government apparatus to expedite approvals.

The good news is that this kind of senior-level intervention is no longer necessary for most businesses to obtain licenses or address a specific regulatory challenge. The bad news is that it has become increasingly difficult to gauge and garner government support as senior government officials – those capable of affecting real and immediate change – have slowly withdrawn from regular interaction with businesses generally, and foreign businesses in particular.

The pace of this change is quickening. The direction in which Xi Jinping is taking China – called "The New Normal" by China watchers – endeavors to make corruption more difficult by limiting the points of direct contact between business and officialdom even further. While this is a net positive for the direction of governance in China, it has left many domestic companies and nearly all foreign companies bereft of a useful channel to combat bureaucratic roadblocks. It also means that it is getting even more difficult to gain any access to government beyond that which is required by law.

The *guanxi* masters fade away

There are still individuals and enterprises operating in China and overseas that preach the gospel of "*guanxi*," the idea that business success in China depends less on *what* you know than on *who* you know. Whatever challenges you face in China, goes the refrain, if you know the right people, the challenges and barriers you face can be eliminated.

During the initial years of China's reforming and opening, when it was essential to gain the trust of key individuals in government merely to be given the right to operate in China, the best of these "China business consultants" provided a genuine service. As the Chinese government began to develop a set of policies and procedures to govern the interaction of business and the government, the usefulness of consultants who could get you a meeting with the Minister went into decline. Today, it is becoming more difficult to justify the costs and risks of engaging such guides, even for companies in the most dire of straits.

To understand this, it is essential to understand the ephemeral nature of "*guanxi*."

Guanxi are personal and unique to the individuals within your organization that have built the relationships. They do not transfer automatically to the company, and unless others in the company have developed similar relationships, they evaporate when the *guanxi* owner departs.

Guanxi are reciprocal: every time that someone in your company reaches out to a government official with whom they have a relationship to pull in a favor, this creates a reciprocal obligation that has to be repaid in the future. At some point, that official will come to your employee and ask for payback.

Further, dependence on relationships with government officials to gain, expand, or hold market access is a perilous stratagem. Your official connection will only stay in his or her seat for a few years. The day will come when he or she will be gone – promoted, perhaps, but more likely transferred, quit to go and work for your competition, retired, sacked for incompetence or corruption, fired for being overly friendly to your company, or (as happens with growing frequency) dead of disease or overwork. As the government's system for working with business becomes more about process than trust, any given official has fewer and fewer levers at his or her disposal to move policy or regulation in favor of a company.

On top of that, each official faces a higher degree of scrutiny over their interaction with companies, which makes it not only difficult to exert influence, but is potentially career-limiting as well. This means that even if you form relationships, they may not be there when you need to tap them.

Finally, *guanxi* are declining in importance as the modus operandi between companies and the government becomes more formal and more distant. What is replacing the old system of trying to move policy through a tenuous series of relationships is a shared and accurate understanding of the environment and of the forces that drive policy, including the levers that drive those forces (in society, industry, and the economy) and the tools available to enterprises for utilizing those levers.

This new approach makes it essential that the former-government-relations-now-public-affairs team shifts its focus away from the care and feeding of *guanxi* to the coordination of the company's effort to understand and influence policy. Gatekeeper no more, the public affairs function becomes about enabling a wider group of executives to effectively engage in the process.

China's policy and regulatory environment

The part of the business context that is framed by the government is what many practitioners refer to as China's "policy and regulatory environment." We will use this term frequently here, so it is worth explaining why we need such an encompassing term rather than something like "regulations" or "policy." This will also explain why public relations activities directed toward the government are addressing a complex audience.

Veteran China-watcher, barrister and policy analyst Jeanne-Marie Claydon-Gescher once explained to me that the Chinese regulatory environment consists of far more than formal laws and regulations; it actually has four components:

Party doctrine: the set of political and economic principles that serve as a set of ideological guidelines for government action;

Regulations: formal statutes enshrined as law as well as formal rules and directives promulgated by various government agencies, normally framed broadly so as to allow for situational interpretation based on variances in government policy;

Government policy: the set of government approaches to specific issues that are the result of party doctrine filtered through the process of accommodating political and economic challenges; and

Administrative interpretation: the process by which enforcement bodies determine how vigorously and under what circumstances a regulation should be enforced based on current government policy.

It is a truism that lobbying *per se* does not exist in China. What should become clear, however, is that the passage of a law is only the first step in the process of establishing the legal parameters for business operations. Those parameters are, in China, in constant flux, making public relations generally – and public affairs specifically – essential to influencing that environment. The four levels of the environment laid out above mean that simple lobbying is replaced by a multifaceted approach to influence the regulatory environment at each level of regulation and enforcement.

It is *essential* that you keep in mind throughout this discussion that we will talk a lot about "the policy or regulatory issue" you are trying to influence. Even if you have no particular regulation with which you have issue, every company has something that must be addressed in dealing with the government at all times: your company's implicit right to operate in China, and the need to continuously demonstrate to the government that your firm is a critical and positive player in the country's economic and commercial milieu. As we continue this discussion, use this as a placeholder when we talk about policy issues if there isn't something else more pressing for your company at the moment.

A framework for public affairs in China

The term "public affairs" means slightly different things in different contexts, but in China it refers to a company's systematic effort to understand, influence, and accommodate the regulatory environment facing its operations in the PRC. That process initially involves helping company leaders understand the government as a key audience, the policy environment as it affects business, and the means available for addressing and influencing the rapid changes in that environment. Thus grounded, public affairs campaigns involve the orchestration of direct relations, influencer advocacy, and corporate citizenship to cement a company's position in China's political economy.

Practically speaking, the public affairs effort in China incorporates five major functions:

1. Research.
2. Policy Analysis and Strategy.
3. Government Relations.
4. Influencer Advocacy.
5. Corporate Citizenship.

Many companies operating in China are accustomed to modest investments in government relations: hiring one or two people with the "right" connections; meeting regularly with key contacts, and getting the CEO to commit time each year to make the rounds with government leaders. Such a tactical approach is a greater effort than many companies undertake, and it is not without rewards.

As noted above, however, the nature of the business environment in China is becoming ambivalent, if not hostile, to foreign companies, despite protestations to the contrary. The changing environment and the alteration of government priorities that are driving it mean that a more holistic approach is essential.

To understand why each of the steps outlined above is important, and to understand how they fit together into a coherent program to secure a company's place in China, let's take a closer look at each in turn.

Research

Public affairs in China involve two primary directional efforts, one passive and the other active. The passive effort involves research and analysis designed to understand the role that the government plays vis-a-vis a company's business in China, the challenges it presents, and the avenues open to address those challenges. The active effort involves outreach to the government (government relations) via diplomatic channels and via influential Chinese third parties who are able to openly engage the government on behalf of a company or its agenda.

In our experience, most executives have little patience for research and analysis. This is understandable: in business we are, by definition, people of action. What is more, understanding the policy and regulatory environment in most Western countries (and in nearly the entire English-speaking world) is a relatively straightforward process. Regulations tend to be detailed and specific; the division of jurisdictions between government agencies is clear; and policy positions and the debates around them are conducted on the public record. Research and analysis thus strike many executives as a glorified means of wasting time.

China, however, presents unique challenges that make research and analysis essential. Companies face a government that has made a fetish of procedural opacity. Regulations are worded to leave broad scope for interpretation in enforcement. Regulatory agencies have broad and overlapping jurisdictions, and policy debates most often take place behind closed doors and through confidential internal correspondence.

This has lead to an extraordinary dearth of information about the direction of policy and regulation in China. While most companies with long histories in China are used to operating in an information vacuum, operating with such uncertainty about the policy environment is dangerous. Planning a program to address and influence that environment without understanding it first is reckless. Research, followed by cogent analysis, is an essential prerequisite to any government outreach program.

It is important to note at this point that such research is rarely best done internally and that it is better to rely on outside resources for the initial process. Internal resources – senior executives, government relations managers – will come with their own connections to – and view of – the government. The result in most cases is a tendency to see the government through the prism of their own connections and experience. However valuable those may be to the company, they result in most cases in a "frog-in-the-well" view of a company's policy environment. To understand the full range of active and latent issues that a company faces, and to avoid getting blind-sided, a company needs a holistic perspective on the policy environment that transcends the perspective of a single individual or of an internal team with personal interests vested in the outcome.

Gathering data is thus best accomplished by impartial experts who are able to provide a view of the government and policy unfiltered by previous impressions and advice: as we go through the kind of information a company needs, the reason for that will become clear. Equally important, policy research in China is a delicate process. The aforementioned government fetish for opacity means that researchers walk a fine line between fair discovery of information on the one hand and what Chinese authorities might interpret as revelation of state secrets on the other. Experienced researchers in China understand how to stay on the safe side of that line while providing deep understanding and actionable insight.

Such research and analysis need not take months and a small fortune to complete. With the right partners engaged and proper guidance, the job can be done in a matter of weeks. The key is knowing what you need to find out, and providing your research partner as much guidance as possible.

Research, whether in an initial project to discover the contours of policy or as part of an ongoing effort, needs to reveal to the greatest extent possible:

- Current party doctrine, to the extent that it affects the policies around business generally and the company in particular. This should include not only current doctrine, but, since that doctrine evolves, political trends and debates that portend change.
- The current direction of broader economic and government policy and how it affects a company's business (the "macro-policy" environment).
- The direction of government policy as it applies to the company, its industry, and its customers, and changes in the role that the government is playing in the company's industry (the "micro-policy" environment).
- An inventory of current and potential issues that could arise for the company out of government regulatory action (a regulatory issues map).
- The full scope of party organs, central government agencies, and provincial and local government bureaus[1] with an interest (or a potential interest) in the company's business (a regulatory roster). This essential step ensures that you capture the entire scope of agencies and officials that for one reason or another might have, might seek to have, or might believe they have some form of jurisdiction over your activities in China. Overlap in jurisdictions[2] is common, exacerbated by regular government reorganizations that redraw the lines between agencies and ministries and leave confusion over exactly who is in charge of what.
- The process by which China's government apparatus creates policy for the company and its industry, and where the points of influence are in that process (a government map). These processes vary by sector, by the ministries involved, and by issue, and are often affected by external policy concerns, so keeping abreast of your relevant policy-making apparatus is a constant challenge.

Once you have captured all of this information into a single place that can be shared with the organization (and any agencies with which you are working), the next step is to turn that research into action.

Policy analysis and strategy

At the very least, the research will reveal several insights. It will likely make clear that you have a wider gamut of regulators than you initially suspected. It will reveal a range of issues that pose a latent, if not immediate, regulatory threat to the smooth operation of the business in China. And it will also demonstrate that addressing the more important issues is unlikely to be easy or quick.

The easy and quick issues do not require a strategy. They are a matter of a phone call, a correctly followed procedure, or a handful of meetings. As they are not issues with which PR needs to be concerned, we will skip over them, with a single caveat: companies operating in China regularly face potentially sticky regulatory situations for which a quick but ethically questionable solution will be proffered. Whatever their other advantages, and the opinion of corporate counsel aside, such solutions should immediately send up public relations red flags. The notion that an unethical act will remain secret because it is either common practice or concluded behind closed doors has been disproven by recent history. Any unethical act vis-a-vis the government or a government official is doubly a latent liability for the company and should be avoided.

That may well shift a "quick issue" into the "hard issue" pile. For those cases, and for all of the regulatory issues that the company faces that cannot be addressed with one or two steps, a more methodical approach is in order. That approach begins with a series of questions, best posed and answered in a four- to six-hour meeting that brings together the company's China leadership team (including functional staff leaders such as the financial director, corporate counsel, and human resources director) and, as an option, more senior executives as well. With the public relations team leader as moderator (or, alternatively, an outside facilitator), the following questions are posed and answered in sequence:

1. What are the three or four most urgent (immediate and impactful) regulatory issues that the company faces?
   Each attendee should provide their list of the top three issues among those that were identified in the research. Based on the team's combined input, the team should agree on the top priorities.
   Then, for each of those issues, answer the following:
2. What is the policy-making process for this issue? This should be clear from the research.
3. Who are the government entities and officials that are involved, and what is their current perception of and bias on the issue? These should also be clear from the research.
4. For each issue, how can we make best use of our potential allies in government to secure a favorable outcome? This will take some interpretation, but will be clear from the research and from internal knowledge.
5. Who are the government entities and individuals that are opposed to a favorable outcome on the issue?
   a. Are they critical players, i.e. can they directly affect the outcome?
   b. If so, can they be influenced?
   c. If so, by whom? Which audiences, if rallied, could move the government on our behalf?
   d. What are the factors that are keeping them from supporting a favorable outcome?
   e. What are the factors that could drive them to support a favorable outcome?

Working through these answers at the very least will frame a set of objectives for a public affairs program. More likely, the exercise will provide a clear set of goals and hint at the outlines of the program itself so you can start to formulate your strategy.

Now that you have identified the government entities that you wish to target, a key to an effective strategy will be deciding the means by which to influence your policy and regulatory environment. There are, essentially three ways to influence policy in your favor, and occasionally a fourth:

1. direct contact and discussions with targeted government officials and entities;
2. diplomatic intercession by the company's home government advocating the desired policy on behalf of the company;
3. activating local influencers and audiences to serve as advocates for the desired policy with the targeted government officials; and, if appropriate,
4. gaining government favor by demonstrating exceptional corporate citizenship.

We will discuss the advantages and disadvantages below as we talk through their execution.

The simplest means to building a strategy is to specify your target audiences to the greatest degree that is practical, to enumerate which (or what combination) of the above four approaches you will use, to set out a time frame, and to state as clearly as possible your objective. As with all good strategies, you should be able to articulate in 20–40 words what you are going to do and how you are going to go about it. Examples of such strategies are:

> Build support over the next year for international online education providers among key policy makers in the Ministry of Education and other government bodies by activating key opinion leaders in China's education space.
> Gain key regulatory approvals within six months for carbon-fiber aircraft by a combination of direct outreach and indirect outreach by local Chinese suppliers and contractors.
> Obtain approvals for the import of US bison products through the establishment of a US Bison Association office in Beijing for

direct outreach, and by making a health-based case in Chinese media for bison consumption in China.

Once your strategy is laid out, it is time to build the campaign. Again, each campaign is as unique as the company for which it is created and the situation that it faces. Nonetheless, there are some common guidelines that will help you ensure that you are building a realistic, effective program.

Direct government outreach

The first and most obvious component of a public affairs program is direct outreach, or what might be more casually termed "government relations." This is the effort of building direct contact and relationships with key government ministries and agencies via the policy makers, regulators, legislators, and procurement executives that make the policy choices. It can also include relevant organs and officials of the Chinese Communist Party, but only on rare occasions when the Party has exercised its privilege to take on direct administration of key areas of regulation (and only then, with great care).

At one point, government outreach was the most logical and effective means to ensure that policy and regulation did not stand in the way of the development of industries and even foreign enterprises. For policy makers, direct contact with senior business executives provided an opportunity to size up companies first hand, to direct their investments, and to gain extraordinary concessions from the world's leading corporations. For senior bureaucrats tasked with creating a modern regulatory framework for entire industries, interaction with foreign enterprises was an invaluable channel of insight in the creation of that framework.

For the reasons noted earlier in this chapter, the opportunities for executives of private and foreign enterprises to meet with and make a case directly to Chinese government officials have

gone from regular to rare. That does not mean that those opportunities will not come along: it simply means that they will be
serendipitous. For that reason, most public affairs plans need
to lay the groundwork for government interaction so that the
company – and its executives – is prepared to make the most of
them when they occur so that each interaction helps move the
case forward.

There are several likely means for a company's executives to
interact with senior policy makers:

1. **Formal meetings:** When we talk about government
   interactions, we are referring most often to formal meetings
   with government officials who have it within their authority
   to either make or advocate polices and regulatory rulings that
   are important to the company. These meetings may be held on
   company premises (for example, as part of an overseas trip)
   but more often are held in the offices of the official in question.
   As noted above, these opportunities are increasingly rare and,
   therefore, each one is potentially more valuable.

2. **Informal meetings:** While formal meetings are considered
   highly desirable, depending on what you are trying to
   accomplish, an informal meeting away from everyone's office,
   for lunch, for dinner, or even for a cup of coffee can be the
   more valuable opportunity. There is a great deal of theatre and
   protocol implicit in formal government meetings, which often
   obstructs meaningful discussions. Informal meetings have the
   advantage of pushing all of that out of the way and allowing
   companies to provide an in-depth briefing to an official (or
   group of officials) on a subject, to have a frank discussion
   about mutual concerns, and build understanding and trust.
   An informal meeting can be even more challenging to set up
   than a formal meeting, but if you have information or insights
   of interest to key officials, it can be a superb forum to provide
   that – and to move things forward. The significant downside is

that officials are unlikely to make formal commitments to any course of action during informal meetings.

3. **Group or association meetings:** The government's growing reluctance to engage directly with individual enterprises has been partially offset by a willingness to work with organized groups or associations of businesses. This is particularly the case when those associations include a fair representation of local Chinese enterprises among their members. This allows officials to take input from industry and enterprises without the taint of favoritism toward a specific company. While it is a little more acceptable to hold these meetings, the downside is that any individual company has limited control over the agenda, limiting their usefulness. What is more, some officials might use such meetings to issue statements or proclamations about a given industry, thus both hijacking the meeting agenda and running the risk of giving the government an opportunity to cast new obstacles in the way. Therefore, before calling together your five closest competitors and setting up one of these meetings, carefully balance the potential risks with the (likely) limited rewards.

4. **Meetings around events:** One reason why events like the annual Boao Forum in Hainan, the Asia-Pacific Economic Coopertion (APEC) meetings that rotate around the region, and the World Economic Forum's Annual Meeting of the New Champions (Summer Davos) are so popular is that these have become one of the last politically acceptable ways for government officials to interact with corporate leaders. There are limits on the number of such events that leaders are allowed to attend, so simply throwing together an industry event and inviting a lot of government leaders will not necessarily grant you audiences. What is more, interaction with leaders is increasingly challenging. Many spend these events meeting with their counterpart from other countries, and operate according to tightly prepared schedules. It is possible (with

considerable effort) to get onto these schedules with a high-profile CEO or founder and something worthwhile (for the official) to discuss. These are valuable and, if nothing else, can be starting points for further interaction.

Regardless of which meeting falls on your schedule, hope for a successful outcome depends less on charm than on timing and superb preparation. Timing is essential: trying to schedule one of these events when the issue you are concerned about has already become the subject of wider political discussion is probably not going to see much progress, even if you get the meeting. Equally, scheduling in the shadow of a national holiday, during a crisis, or during and immediately before the annual meetings of the National People's Congress is difficult and ill-suited to bear substantial fruit. Both the official in question and his or her staff will be preoccupied, so quick follow-up and action resulting from the meeting is unlikely. Schedule your efforts to avoid these events.

Preparation is the second key to success in government meetings. You cannot always control when the government comes calling, nor can you call for a government meeting at just the perfect time. Nonetheless, you always need to be prepared for that call to come. There are several essential steps that should not be forsaken in this process:

Prepare the ground: If you are – or an executive in your company is – about to go into a government meeting and you are reading this to obtain tips, skip this bit and go down to "Get briefed" below. If, on the other hand, you have no meetings on the immediate horizon, you need to do all you can before you start scheduling them to ensure that the person you are meeting with has heard good things about you and/or your policy positions from as many sources that the official trusts as possible in advance. Given how rare (and brief) the meetings with your key regulators will be, the more that the official knows in advance, the better.

In addition to using the indirect influence toolkit (which we will address shortly), this also means reaching out to the official's subordinates and staff and providing them with as much supporting information as possible. It should not be necessary to note that even though a growing number of government officials are multilingual, the official language of China remains Chinese, and you will want to provide as much of your information as possible translated into impeccable Chinese before you provide it to any government office.

Get briefed: Every executive in your company, even those of Chinese background, should be formally briefed before going into a meeting by the individual on the public affairs team most familiar with the official and organization with whom the meeting will take place. The briefing should include a schedule, the biography of the key officials in the room, a rundown of their previously stated positions on and experience with your industry and company, where they sit in the decision-making process, their likely policy goals, and questions they will probably ask. The briefing should fit into a 20–30-minute slot, with questions.

Particularly in the case of executives visiting from outside of China, a face-to-face briefing is not always possible. In such cases, a briefing booklet becomes essential. That booklet should be finalized and in the executive's hands five to seven days prior to the scheduled meeting. As a starting point, it should include:

- a cover page;
- a table of contents;
- a summary sheet that includes scheduling and logistics information;
- a profile of each official known to be at the meeting, including their biography, previously stated positions, experience with the industry and company, and role in the decision-making process;
- expected questions and suggested responses;
- suggested agenda and talking points, cleared (if possible) with the official and his or her staff beforehand;

- notes from prior company meetings with this official, his or her subordinates, or others in the same ministry/agency;
- background materials on where the issue stands in the government generally.

Know your limits: Make sure that any executive going into a meeting with the government is clear about what they should speak about, what they should avoid discussing, what can be promised, what is the most that can be asked for in the discussion, who should take the lead in the discussion, and what time the meeting should end. Also, if there is any form of identification or documentation that the executive will need to bring, make sure that it is prepared in advance.

Prepare a defensible case: It is essential to ensure that your approach is framed in a way that credibly demonstrates – even to the cynical – that the policy you advocate is in China's best interests. Not only does this help your advocates in government dodge accusations of collusion, it also makes it easier for your advocates to build consensus around the policy, and for their successors to sustain the policy long after they have left office.

The key word in that last paragraph was "credibly." If you approach these meetings with messages that offer little more than a positive interpretation of a policy that could have serious negative effects, you are doing neither your company nor its advocates a favor. Come prepared not only with stances but also the evidence and facts to support the policy you advocate, and similarly supported answers to the objections.

Remember protocol: Following a behavioral pattern of their Imperial predecessors, Chinese government and Party officials are sticklers for protocol – in essence, meeting with a person in your organization who reflects the importance of the Chinese official taking the meeting. It would be no more appropriate to send a junior staffer fresh from university to take a meeting with the Minister of Commerce than it would be for the global CEO of a Fortune 500 company to take a meeting with a low-level municipal functionary.

Officials are somewhat less orthodox about this than they were in the past, but it does make sense to ensure that each individual in the company engages with government at the highest level possible without giving offense. Seek out advice from your team, but as a general rule of thumb: global CEOs correspond with full Ministers, city mayors, provincial governors, and city and provincial Party chiefs. Local managing directors correspond with directors general and vice-ministers, vice-mayors, vice-governors, and deputy Party chiefs.

Protocol is rather more relaxed in informal meetings, changing according to the situation, but is not dropped entirely. Always err on the side of formality until advised otherwise by the ranking official in the room, or until it is clear that things have been toned down.

Keep expectations modest: After exerting a great deal of time and effort in obtaining a meeting and bringing a corporate senior executive (or CEO) across an ocean for that meeting, expectations for some sort of "breakthrough" will be high. Keep those expectations in check. A meeting is a meeting, no matter how senior the participants, and the most you should hope for is a casual commitment to advance the cause. Unless you are explicitly promised otherwise beforehand, do not expect more, and above all do not press for more. Leaving your government contacts positively disposed to your company and your point of view will be the most important victory that you can secure. Keep that as your target.

Make it worth their while: Officials do not grant meetings on a whim, and the old habit of scheduling meetings just to "check in" with contacts has largely become a thing of the past. You know what your agenda is: ask yourself what it is that you can offer to the government official that will make the meeting memorable, insightful, informative, and a profitable use of his or her time. Not only will that help you get the meeting in the first place, it will also make scheduling subsequent meetings much easier.

Never say "no": During the course of a meeting with a senior official, it is not uncommon to be asked for a commitment or a concession that you are unable to give, either at that time or ever. No matter how nicely you couch it, you should avoid a flat-out "no" to such requests. The best approach is to ask to hear the rationale for that commitment or concession, and then to note that you can consider the commitment or concession, and will get back to them at a later time.

Have your own translator: Government officials will usually bring their own translators to a meeting: most agencies and ministries have an entire cadre of translators for those purposes. Because of the gradual decline in meetings with international executives, the number of translators – and their relative quality – has declined. Many translators find it more rewarding to leave government service and serve on a freelance basis. You do not want to leave the outcome of your meeting to the vagaries of poor translation. Unless everyone in the room is native fluent in Mandarin Chinese, the best approach is to bring a top-quality translator to double-check the translation provided by the government translator. If possible, have the two translators sit together

Discretion is key: In many cases, particularly if progress in China of any sort is of interest to investors, you will be tempted to publicize the news of a meeting with a senior Chinese official. Resist the temptation. Keep in mind that official meetings with companies (especially foreign companies) are discouraged. Generating a lot of publicity around the meeting could backfire on the official, and could make follow-on meetings more difficult to schedule.

Local vs. national government

Balancing the relative importance of local vs. national governments is as much art as it is science, and while most companies will find that the national government has the most impact on their business, companies in retail, distribution, logistics, and other industries that require the establishment of a network of local offices and infrastructure will find that local government actually takes up the bulk of their public affairs efforts. Indeed, the importance of local governments is not limited to companies with geographically diverse operations.

Here is why: whereas the principles outlined above apply to inter-actions at all levels of government, an important caveat to all of the above is that while all government units at all levels have been told to cut back on meetings with companies (especially foreign firms), it is a general truism that the lower the level, the greater the access. This does not sound like much consolation: if the big decisions are made at the national level, any company, especially a foreign company, would want access at that level.

Yet, as we discuss below about building a "chorus of voices" in support of your policy and regulatory efforts, local governments can be powerful and effective advocates to higher levels of government – even the national government – on your behalf. Time invested in cultivating municipal, district, and even village-level officials can be essential if you find the doors closed in Beijing. For that reason – going local to influence the national – can be a powerful approach for companies, especially those with deep invest-ments in a given locality or operations across wide areas of China.

Another reason why local governments must be addressed is that while policy and regulations set by national governments usually overrule those set at the local level, for many issues – facility-related issues, tax policy, cross-country logistics,[3] and business reg-istration, to name a few – local governments can have considerable say in the success of your business. Reaching out to local officials alongside your partners in each province or municipality can not only go a long way in heading off potential issues, it can also unearth potential opportunities.

Local government is thus not only a potential liability, it is a frequently overlooked potential asset. A public affairs program that does not take these potential advocates into account is missing a significant opportunity.

Corporate diplomacy

A caveat to keep in mind in all government relations efforts is that not all government officials hold a particularly high opinion of public affairs staffers, and as a matter of both pride and protocol they usually prefer to work with senior executives like regional and global CEOs. This underscores an important point: direct interaction with the government should not be the charge of a single individual, nor should it be delegated in its entirety to a specialist department, like human resources. The responsibility for public affairs lies with the senior executive present in the market, supported with the counsel and research of the public affairs team.

Indeed, it is helpful to see the top executive in China as a sort of ambassador, a corporate diplomat who is always ready to represent the CEO of the company in interactions with the government. It is also helpful for company executives coming to China to see their interactions with government in a similar vein. Rather than avoid interaction with the government completely or pursue an independent government relations agenda, each executive should be aware of his or her role in an overall "diplomatic" effort on behalf of the company and its goals in China.

One reason why this is important is that some of the best opportunities to influence the thinking of a government official happen when they are least expected: for example, when a senior company executive is seated next to an official at a dinner or on an airplane, at an embassy reception, or even at an industry functions overseas. All senior company executives need to be prepared for these meetings as far as is practical, even those executives whose purview does not include China.

In support of the "corporate diplomacy" approach, many companies have set up a system – perhaps an all-leadership China conference call – to ensure that all executives are briefed on a quarterly basis. Such a briefing might include a summary of the overall political climate in China, how that climate affects the business, and the regulatory and policy challenges the company faces. It should also include a brief review of the key players who are enablers (or roadblocks) for the company, and how to handle a meeting with a Chinese government official when they meet one (don't push for concessions, commit to nothing, but listen, leave a positive impression, and try to set up for a wider discussion later).

Along similar lines, many companies include a China briefing in the on boarding process for new executives, and for more senior executives, a trip to China. At some point in that process, executives should have a briefing like the one outlined above, as well as be given the background of the company's public affairs efforts and the rationale underlying the approach.

Executives did not get where they are by simply accepting the way things are done at face value, and newly arrived senior executives are likely to have an opinion about the conduct of public affairs. Thus, at some point in this process you are likely to come across dissenting voices. We talk about how to handle these in Chapter 8.

The more that corporate leadership is "with the program" on China, the more effectively the company will be able to capture the full value of the direct relations opportunities that come along, whether planned or unplanned.

Diplomatic intervention

Foreign companies operating in China have access to another public affairs resource: the assistance of the home government as advocates for pro-business policy in China. It is not uncommon for many international governments to expend a considerable amount of time, money, and ambassadorial attention on gaining greater access for their businesses to the China market. In addition, organizations like Australia's AUSTRADE and the US Foreign Commercial Service maintain sizable operations in China with the express purpose of assisting companies from Australia and the United States (respectively) to succeed in China. Both types of resources – diplomatic advocacy and commercial support – are resources for the public affairs (PA) team. At the very least, PR and PA teams should meet and get to know the individuals at the embassies who oversee trade relations, WTO compliance, and commercial support.

Embassies – and the government resources behind them – can provide support to public affairs on several levels. Diplomats can be excellent sources of *information* during the research phase and should have a considerable amount of knowledge of the individuals and agencies in government that have an interest in a company's sector. Beyond the basics, they are also sources of *insight* about current regulatory trends, the state of play in trade negotiations, and the general attitude in the government toward foreign companies. Often information about these topics that is not yet publicly available can be provided to executives who ask about specific issues, and diplomats will often be able to sift through the reams of information generated by the embassy and provide you with research reports that offer insight.

In some cases, embassy staff will be able to help you work around the restrictions that Chinese government officials face in their ability to meet foreign companies by arranging and accompanying you to government meetings. You should use this as a last resort, since a request for a meeting coming from an embassy must take a tortuous course through ministerial bureaucracy on the Chinese side at least, and, depending on your government's current policy, on the home government side as well. Results are not guaranteed, and will probably not be quick, but if a meeting is critical and you have no other means to secure one, this is a potential route.

What home governments can provide in the effort to influence policy and regulation, however, is the intervention of your government on your behalf. Under the right circumstances, in a period of positive relations between China and your home country, and conducted in concert with direct outreach and influencer relations, diplomatic intervention over a matter of policy can be the final push that makes change possible.

Intervention can occur on many levels. Sometimes a simple conversation between an embassy staff member and a junior official in the Ministry of Commerce is sufficient. If there is more at stake, however, a more formal effort may be necessary. It may require an embassy First Secretary to reach out to his or her Chinese counterpart, or even the actions of the Ambassador. The higher you go, the greater the potential impact on policy, but also the greater effort needed to gain a result. If the issue is serious and involves a material breach by China of a signed trade agreement or a violation of China's obligations under the WTO, the matter will likely become part of a larger action.

Keep in mind that the wheels of trade disputes between governments grind with a slowness that is in stark contrast to the speed of commerce. Reaching out to mobilize your home government is like waking a giant, and giants who have just woken up move very slowly. Therefore, if your policy concern involves a short-term opportunity, do not involve the home government with the expectation of a quick result. When confronted with such disputes, the Chinese government's habit is to deny and to delay, slowing things down even further.

There are more caveats. Your home government may consider your concern to be either groundless or too trivial to make it a potential matter of contention between China and your country. If that is the case, the most you can expect from the embassy is sympathy, and you will be cast back on your own devices to provoke policy change. A good approach to address such a pushback would be to form an alliance with similarly aggrieved companies. Governments are more likely to move against China when a larger issue is at stake, and the policy or regulation in question affects an entire industry rather than a single company. Embassies and ministries at home pay attention when rivals set aside differences around an issue, and the combined efforts of multiple firms tend to put the levers of economic diplomacy in motion more quickly. If you are uncomfortable being allies with your competitors, obviously, this is a non-starter, but this has happened in the past to great effect. See the section on below on "Associations."

Further, when turning to the home government for help, choose your battles carefully. Your opportunities to use diplomatic intervention as a tool will be limited. Diplomats have a range of interests they must represent and conflicting interests and demands that they must balance. They're also busy: most diplomats in China are seeing their workloads expand quickly because of China's growing role in the global economy, while budgetary and other constraints keep embassy staff from growing to match the workload. Public affairs teams thus would be wise to see diplomatic intervention as a "single use device" to be used only when all other avenues have been tried, and when the issue at hand presents an existential threat to the company's business in China.

Finally, be aware that diplomatic intervention will cause disruption to your current government relations and will mark you as difficult to deal with. If you aren't getting far with the government by any other means – including the indirect influence areas below – this may not represent a considerable loss. Nonetheless, this is the playground equivalent of running to your mommy: it may solve your problem, but it will not make you any friends. This should be considered before asking your home government to intervene on your behalf.

Influencer advocacy

If influencing policy and regulation via direct contact with the government is becoming more challenging, and diplomatic efforts represent a tool of last resort, then engaging influential third parties to make your case to the government becomes a critical part of your public affairs program. It also solidifies the placement of public affairs under, alongside, or within public relations. The competencies required to move government policy are less akin to traditional lobbying and more like an influencer-based public relations campaign. The toolkits of policy advocacy and corporate promotion have converged.

As you engage with key officials opportunistically and keep the diplomats in your back pocket, the primary means of influencing policy and regulation in support of your business goals will be the "chorus of voices[4]" built by the PR and PA team. That chorus will be specific to your company and to the specific policy issue that you seek to influence. The groups you engage will be those that have much to gain – and possibly more to gain than you – from a favorable policy change, which will make them willing advocates.

Equally important: the advocates you approach must be Chinese. Corraling more foreigners to plead for a policy change on behalf of another foreigner does not strengthen the case. On the contrary, it makes the officials on whom you are focusing feel ganged-up on, and it potentially turns the issue into a "foreigners vs. Chinese" matter. We have seen this happen in China with the issues of intellectual property rights protection, foreign access to the film market, and questions of technology standards. The result has been even more negative policy repercussions because the case for change always came from foreign voices.

Used correctly, the influencer approach has several advantages. It obviates the need to seek out meetings with the government. It allows considerable freedom of action that can help move the matter forward without government involvement. It can serve to improve a company's ties within its ecosystem in China, and in so doing more clearly integrate the company into the commercial and economic fabric of the nation.

From a communications standpoint, local voices in support of a policy change give that change true legitimacy in the eyes of all observers, from the people to the Party. The effort takes place in the marketplace of ideas rather than in closed back-rooms, which deepens the legitimacy of the change and makes it harder to renege in the long run. It takes the company out of the loop, ensuring that the impact of the program is high in proportion to the effort that the company must expend. Finally, it gets other people talking about your company and your goals (always a plus in communications) and it aligns the company with an effort that serves the good of the industry in China.

As with all tactical implementation, the steps you take to put a program like this into action will vary by company and situation. Generally, a good guideline is to use what we call the "4A" approach: Assess, Approach, Assemble, and Activate. In the assessment phase, you decide on the regulatory issue or issues upon which you seek to focus, and the ministries, agencies, and policy makers that will be the target of the effort. You then choose the audiences you want to work with in the effort.

The first and most obvious audiences are the companies who rely on you and the product or service you provide. Approaching local vendors, local partners, and local customers is your initial most important step, as their fortunes are most closely intertwined with your own. They are more likely to see the commonality of interest and work with you as advocates.

At the same time, the government will see that you are mobilizing your ecosystem, but while this is convincing, it is not sufficient in its own right. You will need disinterested third parties to speak on your behalf. Local governments, especially those that are the home for your partners, suppliers, and customers, are strong candidates to be advocates. Leading university professors from the relevant departments of top Chinese universities can be very convincing: China's government is a mix of Confucian and technocratic elements, and the respect for educated experts with PhDs runs deep. A small group of specialists speaking on your behalf can be powerful indeed.

Similarly, there are think-tanks and labs affiliated with either major universities or even government ministries that often serve as close advisors to the government in the formulation of detailed policy. These organizations – like the Chinese Academy of Science, the Chinese Academy of Social Sciences, and the research institutes under the different ministries – are prime interlocutors for conducting indirect policy influence.

A key audience that we mentioned above was that group of government officials who, for reasons not related to any material benefit, are already supporters of your suggested policy change. These officials should be engaged directly if possible and through a partner if necessary, and provided with studies and other support for an effort that they would conduct on your behalf with other government officials.

Once we have assessed the issue and chosen the audiences that we will use to exert influence, we need to assemble a case for each audience that will not only convince them of the fundamental correctness of the policy change, but will also convince their audience. This process involves framing a pitch for each audience that will be sufficient to convince them to begin speaking and will work for them, and assembling the necessary support in the form of studies, cases, and so on to demonstrate the point.

For one client trying to drive the adoption of a technology standard, we reached out to Chinese manufacturers who had been left collectively with a paltry 3% market share because of the control that American and European competitors exercised over the current standard. We were able to make the case to the local manufacturers that, with the new standard, local companies would no longer be at a disadvantage with respect to foreign firms, and indeed would have an opportunity to compete with the Americans and Europeans overseas. This was in fact the way things turned out, but the hook was that the local firms saw the policy change as an opportunity, a chance, to beat the foreigners at their own game. This was enough to turn them into vigorous advocates, and with the support of government think-tanks that could attest to the technology's superiority, the technology was subsequently adopted.

We will talk more about the recruiting of key influencers in Chapter 8.

Now we are ready to approach the audiences. This is best done on a one-to-one basis, because it makes each individual feel like they are playing the critical role in the process. Only if it is absolutely impractical due to time constraints to conduct a one-to-one effort does it make sense to reach out to your audiences as a group. When doing so, though, you need to ensure that you are not putting competitors into the same room and that you are not mixing up commercial, academic, and government audiences. These are all best kept as separate as possible.

Once you have made the initial approach, activate your advocates by following up regularly with additional facts and information that will help the cause. But do not push. The idea is to make each individual in the process feel the imperative to act on their own. Your job is to serve as facilitator, coordinator, and information source – no more.

In any given group you will have a number of people who will do nothing. The Pareto principle applies here: you will get 80% of your results from the most proactive 20% of your audience. One client asked me why it wouldn't be simpler and quicker to find two or three really influential people to make the case for you and not go through the trouble of building support across a range of audiences. It is a fair point: if there are two or three people that you can identify who can not only bring about the policy change you require but also ensure that it won't be overturned by someone else in 18 months, by all means engage them and move on. If you are like most foreign companies operating in China, chances are that two to three people with that range of capabilities and that are open to speaking out on your behalf simply don't exist. But most important, with only two to three people, there is no room for a Pareto effect, and the possibility that you will have three advocates who are doing little or no advocacy is high. You should reach out to as wide a group as possible so that in reality you can afford for one advocate out of five to be carrying the bulk of the effort forward.

Associations

Another means of exerting indirect influence is by working through industry associations, allying with other companies in your industry or ecosystem, even competitors, in the effort to guide policy makers. Similar to the influencer advocacy approach, banding together not only serves to amplify your voice on an issue, it also raises it above the level of proprietary concerns and makes it larger: the sight of rabid competitors in an alliance makes a strong statement. This is particularly the case if those competitors include local companies.

This approach, pioneered by APCO and Burson-Marsteller in the late 1990s, has now been widely adopted. Associations can be local representation of global industry groups, locally created groups, or Chinese industry associations that also include international businesses.[5] These associations can be general industry associations, focused on issues of wide interest, or they can be built around specific issues. Ideally you would work with an association that is already in place, but if that is not possible, the best way to organize an association is to appoint an agency or another neutral third party to serve as the organizing unit. The agency would provide coordination and manpower, and help guide the discussions of the organization.

Initial discussions should be kept informal, with the goal of building consensus on goals and agreeing on an approach. For an association already in place, and with all legal certifications from the government, it is possible to reach out as an association. Otherwise, it is best that the group serves only to coordinate the separate outreach efforts of all of the companies involved: the Party can be quite sensitive about the formation of ad-hoc groups for political purposes. The key is for the government to be hearing from all quarters of the industry that the policy needs to be created or altered.

If one level of coordination of the group is message (what to say), the other level of coordinating an industry association is targets (to whom to deliver the message). Each company reaching out to the government should share which officials they are approaching so as to avoid crossed wires. Post-meeting feedback should be solicited and shared to that progress can be noted and next steps planned.

One additional note about associations: It is a favorite tactic of the government when faced with outside groups to want to play "divide and conquer." The best groups take this into account from the beginning and work to ensure that everyone shares the same goals for the same reasons. Use care: if one or two key competitors can be induced to throw in the towel for a preferential concession, everyone is sunk, and you may wind up with a worse situation than before. At least one individual – preferably a charismatic CEO or China general manager – should be entrusted with keeping the effort united. This issue of coordination suggests that an association approach can be a powerful tool, but only if everyone at the table is equally threatened by the policy at hand.

Corporate citizenship

Influencers as advocates on your behalf, supported by associations and your own direct contacts with the government form the troika of your public affairs program. There is one other element that deserves mention, and that is the issue of corporate citizenship.

A number of companies have tried to build influence with the government generally and with specific regulators through acts of outstanding corporate citizenship designed to prove that, by virtue of its civic-mindedness, the company has earned the right to be a part of China's economy. These efforts range from conducting corporate social responsibility (CSR) efforts to the establishment of R&D facilities in China.

Generally speaking, these efforts do not yield tremendous results with the government. As one Chinese official put it at a conference in Beijing several years ago, as far as the government was concerned, a foreign company – indeed any company – was doing all it needed vis-a-vis corporate citizenship if it followed the law, paid its taxes, and treated its workers well.[6]

Corporate social responsibility remains a challenging topic in China, in particular following the accession of Xi Jinping to the nation's leadership. It is core to the legitimacy of the Party and the government that they be the only sources of social benefits outside those specifically required of a company. Beijing will rarely object when companies step in to support schools in impoverished areas or contribute cash or in-kind donations to disaster relief. But for some less-secure government officials there is an unmistakable whiff of paternalism in such efforts that suggests that these things are being supplied because the Party has somehow failed to do so.

This is not to suggest that you withhold heartfelt and genuine efforts to help improve a bad situation, as long as the CSR is conducted for its own sake. A good rule of thumb is that for acts of philanthropy or community relief, companies should behave toward their community in China the same as they would at home.

Just expect the most heartfelt CSR effort to be viewed by government officials with gentle cynicism. It's not you – it is the corpus of companies that have in the past used some form of CSR as a means to try to influence policy. As such, you should not expect that CSR will help you make headway with the government: if you do, you are likely to be disappointed. Be genuine and conduct the effort without consideration for what it will buy you, and it will buy you more than you think.

As to the opening of research and development labs, this was much the rage right around the turn of the century. That rage has died down. So many R&D centers were set up in such a short time that the effort was no longer special. Worse, there were companies whose R&D was either very low-value work or pure localization, thus failing to yield the benefits of a true R&D center (experienced basic researchers, significant patent portfolios, etc.). Finally, we are now at the stage where Chinese companies are setting up their own R&D networks, and several, including Chinese search giant Baidu and mobile telecommunications leader Huawei, have set up huge R&D facilities of their own overseas, including in Silicon Valley.

In the course of your operations, however, you may discover an opportunity to significantly alter or enhance the operating standards of the industry in China in a way that inspires other companies to follow suit. If you can do something like this, do it because it is the right thing to do, not to gain credit. If you can, find a way to share credit with key government officials, and then make sure that you publicize your action to a wide but appropriate set of audiences.

Corporate citizenship, done for its own sake, will always be an asset, but you should not rely upon it to secure for your company a lasting place in China's economy.

China government relations with home government

As you conduct your efforts to address the Chinese government, it is important to bear in mind that public affairs are becoming increasingly integrated across markets. It may once have been the case that what a company said to the Chinese government, or how it represented itself to government officials in China, had little or no effect on its standing with the government back home. That is most assuredly no longer the case.

As we will discuss in the next chapter, information about a company's operations and actions in China now flows easily across national borders, thanks to the internet and to the vast international news gathering organizations at work in China. As a group of large US internet companies discovered in the first decade of this century, Congressional committees have become adroit at discovering how US firms behave toward the Chinese government, and a company's behavior in China can and will be used against it at home.

This can make things touchy. While messages about sustainability, well-treated workers, and the quality of your innovative products resonate in both places, much of what the Chinese government needs to hear would fall flat at home. When you say, for example, the company will operate in conformity with local laws in every market in which you operate, you make a Chinese official happy and a legislator at home deeply concerned.

This means great care must be used with creating your public affairs plan, when developing messages, and when handling crises. Your PA plans must serve all masters, so make sure you are addressing them at the very earliest moment in the process. Nobody wants to come up with a superb Chinese PA plan that works brilliantly, only to have it buy you a trip to a Senate hearing room.

China government relations and your other publics

There is one last elephant in the room that needs addressing: the ethics of public affairs. Whether through direct lobbying or indirect communications, the idea of a company influencing the policy of any government, even a foreign government, does not go down well among the citizens of free and open societies, and we can expect that Chinese audiences would be equally discomfited if they felt that their government operated at the behest of multinational corporations (it doesn't, but the appearance is bad enough). The recent economic downturns were accompanied by allegations of commercial–governmental collusion on a vast scale. China has not escaped the growing worldwide disgust and discomfort with undue commercial influence on government policy, and it is coming from both the Party and the people.

In order to avoid being accused of relying on back-room deals for your success in China, it is worth considering the following five guidelines as you build your approach to public affairs:

1. **Transparency to the greatest possible extent:** This means standing up in public and telling the world exactly what you

are telling the government, and why. The agenda must be in the clear and open to both scrutiny and debate, as should be the tactical approach the company is taking. This also means that public affairs become more than a matter of speaking to government officials about company input on policy: PA means involving the public as well.

2. **Behavior and actions that withstand public scrutiny:** The public is going to find out what you are doing to influence the process. In addition to making clear what you intend to do, conduct yourself in the process as if a hostile documentary filmmaker was following you around with a camera. Forget chummy dinners and back-room deals. When you are influencing public policy, you are going about the public's business, and you need to behave accordingly.

3. **Avoid behavior for which others have received opprobrium or censure:** If someone else has done it before and gotten in trouble for it, why are you taking the risk?

4. **Avoid all forms of corruption:** Whether your company operates under the aegis of the Foreign Corrupt Practices Act or its counterpart statutes from other countries, you are tainted irrevocably when you use money inappropriately to secure your market position. *Don't do it.* Just because something is permissible doesn't make it right in the eyes of your publics. The more you use money to influence the process, the more liability you are building in the bank of public opinion, and in China you can be assured that eventually a reckoning will come.

5. All of this means you will have to **create a new set of tactics and techniques** for conducting government relations. The way to start the process is to find a way to align your interests with those of the public at large, and keep them there. This will not be easy, but we have ample examples in the history of business to prove that it is not only possible, it is the best way to do business.

Nine public affairs essentials: avoiding trouble

We have covered a lot of ground in this chapter, and there is much to remember and implement. In the meantime, keep in mind the following key rules that, if followed, should help you avoid 90% of the potential problems you would face with the government.

- **No politics**: Keep your organization and its leaders clear of domestic politics in China beyond what you need to do to stay open and operating.
- **No surprises**: Do not let the government, and especially those officials with closest purview over you and your industry, be surprised by anything that you do. Make every effort to keep the government appraised when you are making a major move with your business.
- **Understand the priorities** of your regulators, and given those priorities, be the "partner of choice" in helping to bring their goals about.
- **Do not be obsequious**: The key to all of this is to walk a fine line. You do not want to be branded as a sycophant, sucking up to the government so as to merit their gifts. Facebook's Mark Zuckerberg discovered how this could backfire
- **Speak with a single voice**: Consistency across all audiences is essential, and if you are caught speaking out of both sides of your mouth to different audiences, you will lose your credibility with the government at the very least. And it could get much worse than that.
- **Maintain control over your communications**: Do not allow local partners to take over your communications. Your independent and strong voice with the government will ensure that they understand that you stick to principle above all else.
- **Stay accessible**: Make sure that the government always has someone in China that they can reach out to if they need to contact you officially in a time of crisis, and make sure your key

regulators always know who that person is and where to find them.

- **Approach PA strategically, not tactically**: Follow the guidelines above before framing your plan.
- **Finally, remember that PA has three major roles**: Keeping channels with the government open, making sure that the company does not get blindsided by a sudden change in policy or leadership, and building a broad base of support for the company among influential communities. Do those things, and you will be a high-performing team.

chapter 3

Working with the Media in China

We spend a great deal of time looking at other publics in this book, but your most important influencers – the public that has the most regular impact on your key audiences – is still the legion of reporters and editors working for Chinese print, radio, television, and online outlets. The key is to work with journalists so that they motivate those publics whose actions directly impact a company's business.

In the first two decades after reforming and opening, Chinese journalists earned a reputation among PR professionals for being passive. Little wonder: journalism in China prior to the late 1990s was still largely a matter of reporters filling a daily copy quota. Investigative reporting was unknown, and most editors and journalists were trained to be little more than copywriters for the Party's propaganda organs. For reasons we will go into later, this has all changed. Journalism in China has evolved alongside the nation's media environment. While there are still old-school Chinese journalists who will run a corporate press release as a story in return for a few hundred Renminbi (RMB), that particular species is being replaced by more professional and more specialized reporters in newsrooms around China.

Why pay attention to the Chinese media?

In a world where traditional media is in decline, the internet is increasingly strong, and a growing number of people are relying upon social media as their news aggregation sites, making a case for traditional media seems anachronistic. Coming from a public relations executive, it comes across as so much self-serving prattle.

Yet while in most of the world the rise of the internet and social media has led to a decline (if not outright crash) in traditional media, in China something quite unique has occurred. Since the mid-1990s, traditional media and new media have both been expanding at breakneck speed, and for a range of reasons, traditional media remain an essential, critical part of a company's success in China.

Traditional media in China is healthy

The inflow of advertising is an important reason why traditional media remains relevant in China. A mere trickle in the 1980s, ad revenues have since turned into a cascade of cash. Advertisers spent over US$42 billion in advertising in China in 2012, a total that is expected to rise nearly 11% per year to over $64 billion in 2016,[1] far exceeding the anticipated 7–7.5% growth rate in the overall economy.

Those taps are likely to stay open. Aside from organic growth and the fact that a third of China's population remains offline, several micro factors are contributing to the resilience of traditional ad spend. One is the natural conservatism of senior executives and the cautious, deferential approach marketers take to non-specialist CEOs when it comes to marketing spend. While in most Western companies decisions about where to spend marketing funds (if not the actual size of marketing budgets) is left to senior marketing executives, Chinese CEOs tend to retain final approval power over a far more detailed level of marketing spend. This makes the marketers themselves more conservative. A relatively unsophisticated boss will tend to push his or her team to commit to media he or she consumes, understands, and is comfortable with, and the team will often comply on the theory that nobody ever got fired for buying the media that the CEO prefers.

One last factor works to keep traditional media flush: corruption. There is a longstanding practice among many Chinese media to compensate with kickbacks marketing managers and other decision makers who commit to ad buys. The payola can take different forms, ranging from cash to merchandise, expensive luxury goods and overseas shopping trips.[2] That traditional media are apparently more likely to be able to afford to pay such kickbacks, and thus more likely to pay them, helps ensure that factors other than effectiveness drive advertising decisions, thus prolonging the "happy time" for traditional media in China.

Chinese media has adapted to the internet

Because traditional media and online media have matured together, many of the nation's best media companies have become hybrids. Phoenix TV, China's nominally independent television broadcaster, was among the first traditional media companies in China to leap into the online sea with something more than just an ancillary effort. The company has built what is arguably China's best online news site, branded iFeng, with over a dozen specialty channels along with its main news feed. Similarly, Sina.com has become more than a portal or service provider – it has developed a fully-fledged news gathering organization of its own that easily rivals some of China's largest newspapers and TV stations. While looking like new media companies on the outside, iFeng, Sina, and similar outlets operate their journalism operations in a manner that makes them indistinguishable from traditional media outlets.

Chinese media still owns key audiences

All of this is interesting, and suggests that the Chinese media and the battalions of journalists that they employ will be around for some time to come. But are people consuming them, and does their importance justify the cost of engaging them?

The answer is "yes, for the foreseeable future." The flow of advertising cash has allowed media to invest heavily in upgrades, promotion, and editorial resources (read: "lots of journalists") that have helped the traditional media hang onto some critical audiences. Executives and consumers over the age of 45 still use traditional media as their primary source of information. And unlike their counterparts abroad, Chinese media were quick to cotton onto the internet, and invested early and heavily in online publications even as they built out their print and broadcast capabilities, which has slowed the outflow of readers, listeners, and viewers.

Longer term, say by 2024, demographic trends and the technological evolution of media will likely push traditional Chinese media and news organizations into a spiral of shrinkage similar to the maelstrom that has ravaged media in the developed world. If the political uncertainty around China's future, which hovers like a specter over China's media environment, should turn Party leadership against China's relatively freewheeling media industry, the stroke of a pen could re-institute the draconian journalistic controls that would fairly disembowel China's media sector overnight.

In the meantime, though, the domestic audiences alone make engaging Chinese journalists, editors, and their media essential.

Decision makers are still reading

Part of what my firm and many of our clients do is research the media consumption habits of business leaders. What we find consistently is that, as a rule, people born after 1980 (especially those living in cities) are eschewing magazines, newspapers, and broadcast television in favor of social media, streaming video, online publications, web portals, and (as they acquire cars) broadcast radio.

On the far side of this stark gap, however, sits an audience that has more wealth, discretionary income, and both commercial and political power. While most are online to one degree or another, media habits die hard, and these influential and spendthrift consumers still rely on newsprint and the TV screen.

Unparalleled reach

For all of the copy and attention that has been lavished on how large China's internet has become, and despite exceptions like Sina and iFeng, few sites can match China's traditional media in the breadth of their audiences. The media properties with the most consistent reach remain in the traditional media: television (particularly China Central Television), the leading metropolitan daily newspapers, and websites that essentially act as electronic versions of newspapers and magazines. These are not undifferentiated general channels, either: the simultaneous growth of specialty magazines and the internet have driven a remarkable diversity in the niches covered even by large outlets. CCTV has gone from one to over a dozen specialized channels. Major newspapers offer sections ranging from lifestyle and sports to sustainability and technology. And the addition of the web has allowed these mainstream mass media to slice their massive audiences even more thinly. Audiences – and advertisers – have responded enthusiastically.

The world is reading

Another reason that Chinese media remains critical to public relations in China is that its reach is no longer limited to China alone. In the "old days" (circa 1995), there existed a sort of invisible membrane that separated Chinese media from the rest of the world. Chinese publications were not widely distributed overseas, the language difference made them difficult to access, and there was little interest outside of China in the daily output of Beijing's propaganda machine.

Recognizing the interest that the world now has in China – and, in the case of government media, seeing an opportunity to influence global opinion – some of the larger media outlets have begun translating a growing portion of their content into foreign languages, including English. Media that function as an extension of the CPC and government information organs have spearheaded the effort: Party mouthpiece *People's Daily* has long supported the English language *China Daily* as the country's official newspaper to the world; and CCTV now operates a raft of channels aimed at non-Chinese and overseas Chinese alike. Media operating with a greater degree of independence from the Party, including the powerhouse newsweeklies *China Economic Weekly, Caijing* and *Caixing*, are now producing translated editions and are marketing them with growing skill overseas.

Beyond these sources, Western journalists in China are increasingly bilingual and are drawing information from local outlets. Some of the larger news gathering organizations, including Bloomberg, Reuters, Dow Jones and other wires, employ people or services in China that do nothing but scour the local media for stories related to international companies, listed Chinese firms, and stories that are relevant to global industry and finance. This means that what happens in China is heard around the world, and due to the vagaries of time differences, stories drawn out of the Chinese media tend to hit the wires as London traders have lunch and New York brokers turn on *Squawk Box*.

All told, Chinese media have now acquired a vast secondary following overseas that, in some respects, is even more important than its slowly dwindling domestic audience. Given that anything coming through China's traditional media carries the implicit approval of the Chinese authorities, the coverage carries a value beyond its content. My old mentor, Susan Tomsett, put it this way: China moves markets. What she meant was that *Chinese media move markets*.

Tomorrow's influence

The rise of specialized publications for both consumers and industry has, in turn, enabled the emergence of a class of journalists who make a career out of covering niche and specialty markets. They not only file their daily stories; they also write books about their niches, go on talk shows, and in effect become experts and analysts in their own right. There is a relatively small number of people like this, but their ranks are growing, and if the area of expertise of one of these super-journalists touches on a company's business, it is essential to engage them both as journalists and as budding opinion leaders.

China's media landscape

As the above suggests, the media sector in China has exploded, growing from a handful of propaganda outlets tightly controlled by the Party to a genuine industry with over 10,000 print media, hundreds of radio stations, and over 700 television stations, all in the space of two decades. Addressing this mass can be unnerving for even the most experienced PR hand. The first step in taming Chinese media is to start breaking it down into its component parts, seeking out that handful of outlets that is truly essential to your PR effort.

At the most superficial level, China's domestic media environment is not dissimilar from that of the West. As a whole, Chinese media fall into some clear categories.

There is a robust print media, arguably more vibrant than in the West, where the internet has taken its toll on print and television alike. The healthiest print media are arguably the **newspapers** in major metropolitan areas. *Beijing Evening News, Shanghai Morning Post,* and the *China Youth Daily* China seek out a specific audience. *Beijing Youth Daily*, despite its name, focuses on the capital's professionals, managers, and bureaucrats ranging between 30 and 50 years of age. *Southern Daily* is a national broadsheet that uses its base in Guangzhou to launch edgy and often contro-versial investigative coverage. Regional *Shoppers Guides* are both news outlets and resources for China's consumers. The venerable *Guangming Daily* prides itself as the preferred read of the capital's intelligentsia, and *Wenhui Bao* aims to be the thinker's daily in Shanghai.

General interest **weeklies** are growing in popularity, especially among city dwellers who don't have time to pour through a stack of newsprint each weekday. Led by publications with a strong independent streak like *Southern Weekend, Xinmin Weekly*, and *Beijing Weekly,* these publications offer investigative and long-form stories, weekly news summaries, and arguably some of the best business coverage in the country.

When we talk about **tabloids** in China, we refer more to their con-tent than their printed format. This is perhaps the largest category of dailies. Lacking government support and the resources to com-pete with the nation's leading papers in investigative journalism, they build their readership on a steady stream of sensationalism with Chinese characteristics. Taking care to operate well within government strictures, these outlets specialize in business scandals (especially when they involve foreign businesses), slightly salacious content, and, lately, a particularly Chinese brand of yellow journalism.

Lifestyle media is the newest, fastest-growing, and probably the second-largest segment of Chinese media. This category encompasses everything from magazines aimed at women, such as *LOHAS*, to *National Geographic Traveler*. The sector owes its start to the hardy pioneers of foreign publishers like Hearst, who brought glossy fashion titles such as *Vogue, Elle,* and *Cosmopolitan* to China and set off a mad rush of readers, advertisers, and imitators. In this politically innocuous sector, publications have largely operated well outside the sphere of government oversight, and it is common for editors and even publishers to have no Party affiliation.

Perhaps nothing demonstrates China's departure from its communist roots better than the quality of the **business publications** in the country. Titles like *Economic Daily, China Business News,* and the *21st Century Business Herald* have gradually built positions in the market that mirror those of Western publications like *The Economist, The Wall Street Journal,* and *The Financial Times*. While coverage remains primarily focused on business and economy pieces, these publications will occasionally run in-depth investigative features that can reach into wider topics of interest. For most companies, business publications will show up on the radar at some point; however, be aware that restrictions on political reportage in China mean that the better investigative journalists in China do not cover a political beat, but instead will focus on exposing shocking or illegal business practices. Since such stories are politically acceptable to the government, business media wind up with a disproportionate concentration of China's toughest journalists.

The sheer size of the market in China has enabled the growth of **specialty consumer publications** on a scale similar to that of the United States. Almost every imaginable interest has a publication, sometimes online only, sometimes print only, and most often offering both. Enthusiasts of everything from yoga to military collectibles to photography have a range of publications from which to choose. Travel, entertainment, electronics, real estate, film, automotive, gaming, sports, and health are popular categories; and as niches grow, even more specialized publications appear.

Specialized business and industry publications have emerged alongside their consumer counterparts. China's **trade** media began as a series of dry industry- and trade-specific technical journals produced by the government ministries from which China's state-owned sectors sprang. Driven by the growth in business-to-business advertising and a demand for information among rapidly evolving industries, China's trade media now sports titles from a host of local media groups as well as global publishers including International Data Group (IDG), Global Sources, and CMP Media.

As online video has grown in popularity, China's **television stations** – nearly all of them state-owned – have responded by diversifying their offerings and expanding their channel line-ups. Channels generally fall into one of two categories: those that offer a mixed format but a wider reach (such as CCTV-1), and those that offer specialized formats with tighter audience targeting (CCTV's business and economy channel and Phoenix InfoNews, for example). Viewership, particularly among the young, continues its slow shift to online video, but for the time being TV remains the best medium to reach a lot of people quickly.

China does not have the plethora of **newswire services** that we enjoy in the West, but the home-grown New China News Agency, known by its Chinese hypocorism Xinhua, feeds into nearly every publication in China and carries with it the authority of the Party propaganda organs to which it reports. International news agencies are also active in China, primarily in delivering China content to overseas audiences, but that is starting to change around the edges. Local reporting by correspondents of Reuters, Bloomberg, Agence France-Presse (AFP), the Associated Press (AP), and IDG News Service finds its way into Chinese publications – we will talk more about them below – and provide Chinese readers with a quiet counterpoint to Xinhua coverage.

Finally, but by no means least, are **online media** whose approaches to both news gathering and publishing reflect the traditional media, except that they publish constantly throughout the day. Sina.com, Sohu.com, and Netease.com all began their lives in the mid-1990s as online portals in the Yahoo! mold, but quickly evolved beyond that into organizations that used their own content to drive hits. Each has built a news gathering organization on a par with some of China's leading newspapers, and their reporters are a fixture at nearly every major event. iFeng, the online arm of the Phoenix television empire, represents the most adroit adaptation of television to the internet in China, and as a result offers superb multimedia coverage of subjects in the country. These outlets are joined by a dozen similar online media and literally hundreds of online-only specialist publications that are beginning to dominate their exclusively offline rivals in reach and credibility.

The evolution of the Chinese journalist

As China's media landscape has evolved, so have the journalists. While a casual observer would still note significant differences in journalistic rigor when comparing Western and Chinese journalists, the current crop of reporters and editors represent a noteworthy leap forward over their predecessors. Thirty years ago, a Chinese journalist was essentially a propaganda copy writer. As recently as 20 years ago, many journalists were ticket punchers, hired to fill space in government-subsidized publications that boasted vast readerships simply because there was not much in the way of competition for the people's attention.

That began to change in earnest with both the growth of the internet, which placed a premium on the ability to assemble stories quickly and thoroughly, and with the government's decision in the early 1990s to begin weaning most of the media off the Party's purse. The latter is likely the more important factor in the professionalization of journalism. The growing demand for new and better media – and the rising costs of production – was draining government coffers even as China's development was raising demand for advertising. To assuage the concerns of more conservative Party leaders, a system of editorial supervision overseen by the Party propaganda office was put into place to ensure that all licensed news outlets (and there were none that were not licensed) published only content that met Party approval. This mechanism not only allowed the commercialization of government media outlets, it also served to streamline the reporting process and to set in place a system that would allow new media outlets to develop and flourish.[3]

The downside to all of this was that the media could no longer depend on Beijing for help if the money ran out. Thrust on their own devices, publications adapted quickly to the need to engage readers first and seek ad revenues later. Many publications before and since discovered that solid journalism backed by deft editing and a visionary publisher were the ticket to prosperity. This was the road followed by publications like *Caijing, Caixing,* and China's leading business publications.

But not every media outlet was willing or able to take the high road. The middle road went to the organizations that decided to maintain quality journalism, but focus on a narrower section of the audience. Some publications became highly specialized, and it was this group that formed the basis of the specialty and trade magazine business.

The low road – the descent into the gutter of what charitably can be called "tabloid journalism," was for many publications the easiest answer. Editors understood that sensationalism sells irrespective of culture, and China's embryonic code of journalistic ethics and its nascent libel and slander laws opened the door to an explosion of this type of journalism. As competition intensified, some sank even further: China has been wracked by high-profile cases of media outlets having their journalists threatening to run damaging stories unless the media were paid off in either advertising commitments or cash payments. While the Party has moved to clean up such practices, the ranks of marginal media outlets continue to grow, suggesting that they will be with us for some time to come.

Working with Chinese journalists

Now that you have an idea of whom you are facing and why, it is time to take a look at how you can successfully manage and direct your interaction with them. We'll start with the Chinese media, as they are most important, and will discuss foreign correspondents below.

While journalism in China has evolved to be a much more diverse craft than it was previously, it is still possible to lay out some common guidelines for working with reporters regardless of background. First, while hardly "independent" in the Western sense, journalists value their freedom from interference to the extent that it is available to them. In the past, when a journalist published (or was preparing to publish) a negative story about a company, it was possible for that company to reach out to the government for help in quashing the story. Except in the case of egregious falsehoods that would damage the Party or powerful Chinese entities in the process, that path is no longer available to foreign enterprises, and even

local- and state-owned firms are discovering
that the government is loathe to pressure
journalists off a story. Not only is it a lot
of trouble, but also the government
appears to place growing value
on the role of the media as a
watchdog   over   business,
a kind of auxiliary regulator.

Similarly, the days of "friendly media"
appear to be coming to an end. It used
to be fairly common for journalists to work closely with one or
more companies, serving as their eyes and ears and often their voice
through their writing. This was not necessarily for illicit reasons:
some journalists were simply fanboys and fangirls of the company in
question, and enough readers shared that point of view that it was
not considered a problem. As journalists professionalize there is still a
cadre of reporters building careers by covering one company or even a
handful. But these reporters are less likely to be fans, and more likely
to be balanced – if not critical – in their portrayal of the company.

Always try to build a strong relationship with the journalist (and,
if possible, his or her editor), but do not expect that to buy you a
free ride. Keep in mind that few are genuinely out to get you, and
most simply want to get their job done; but if they see you as a
barrier to that, they will behave accordingly.

Even in the cases of reporters who are trade specialists in your
business, it is safe to assume that the media are operating at a
disadvantage. Usually journalists have only the most superficial
idea of what a company does, and a surprising number of
journalists will show up for an interview or a press conference
having done very little background research about it. Such cases all
offer a superb opportunity to solidify a relationship by providing
not just messages about the company, but by offering genuine

insights about the industry and the sectors it touches through its customers, suppliers, and partners. For example, you will occasionally get a question that sounds silly, or perhaps even quite ignorant, from a reporter, suggesting that they do not understand something very basic about the company and its business – or are, at least, pretending not to understand. These opportunities are golden: few journalists outside of trade publications are likely to understand your business, and sometimes a "dumb question" is a veiled invitation to become a reporter's guide through the complexities of an industry. If you do find yourself in that position, recognize that most reporters (and most people, really) are usually so grateful that you took the time to help (rather than snort in derision and point them toward the company website) that you will find yourself having built a nice pool of goodwill.

Providing such insights can be essential for another reason, which is to avoid having to defend the honor of your proprietary information in the name of a good story for a reporter. Chinese media will certainly dig for facts, but often they are pursuing key financial information or other sensitive data that may not be publicly released. The most common questions asked of international companies are about finances – in particular information about the size and success of your operations in China. In all of these cases it is essential to stick to publicly released information: proprietary facts and figures can often be of aid and comfort to competitors, and for public companies disclosure of its finances outside of the established channels can embroil the company in legal trouble. In all cases, journalists are looking for something that will sell papers or move markets, so make sure everyone is clear about what can be disclosed and what cannot.

The key for every journalist in China is cooperation – responsiveness, insightful information, and access, access, access. Nearly all journalists in China will request greater access to senior executives. Pitching a story, you may find them requesting an interview with an executive as a condition for running the piece. Promise nothing you are not 100% certain you can deliver, as promising something and then reneging is the kiss of death with a reporter in China. The best approach – and one that is acceptable to a surprising number of journalists in China – is the e-mail interview, which we will discuss below.

Responsiveness will be key because nearly every journalist, even those working for long-lead consumer specialty publications, is time-constricted. As is the case elsewhere, the news cycle for Chinese journalists has been compressed from days down to minutes. Journalists have no control over deadlines, and time pressure is so acute (and journalistic standards so rudimentary) that they are more interested in filing on time than getting the story right.

And while Chinese journalists are more likely than their Western counterparts to work from an angle provided to them by a public relations person, chances are they are coming to the table with an angle or a headline in mind. Unless that angle was assigned by an editor, there is some flexibility, and if you are able to work with the reporter early enough in the story development phase and at the end of the process as well, you may have an opportunity to demonstrate to the reporter that there is a better, more insightful angle.

Responding to the media in China

If your company has a high profile in China, it is fairly likely that your first dealings with the media will be responding to inquiries and helping the company start to manage its media interactions in a more systematic way. In an environment where the media are growing quickly and are highly competitive, the first thing you are going to need is a filter, and that begins with a media list.

The fastest way to build a list of media that have an interest in your company and sector is to engage an agency. The advantage of working with an agency – at least initially – is that they are likely to know the media you want to reach. When you hire an agency, make it clear up front that one of their first deliverables will be a media list. Not only does that ensure that you are looking at the entire media universe from the beginning, it also makes the agency reach out to all of the media at the very start, verify their information, and subtly make your company's presence known to media who would have an interest.

Some agencies are reluctant to part with their contacts for free, or cheaply, or early in the relationship with the client. If you have an agency that treats their media list as a proprietary resource – or you are not yet ready to hire an agency – you will need to do some spade work to find the media with the greatest interest in your company.

The first step is just to answer the phone. If you are getting calls from media, chances are they belong on your media list. This does not mean that the people who call you get priority – all too often the most important media do not call you. Nonetheless, the intrepid journalists belong on your list just so that you know who they are.

The second step is to do an online search for stories about your company, its products, its industry, and its competitors. If you are searching in Chinese, naturally, Baidu or Qihoo are likely the best search engines. Make sure that you have all the alternative Chinese spellings for your name – even if you have an official Chinese name, reporters and others often create a phonetic transliteration for your company or product name in China. The Ford Focus, for example, is formally the Fu Shi Kang, but users call it the Fo Ke Si or simply Xiao Fu. Knowing such nicknames is essential for your search, as they will lead you to the reporters already covering you.

Finally, there is what I call the "press release radar." If your company has a relationship with a PR newswire, it can be very helpful for distributing your news releases in China and providing reports on which publications (and sometimes, which reporters) picked up the release. Run through a series of releases – perhaps three to five – and you should have a good list of media with an interest in your company; and for the cost of a headline search, you can get the name of the reporter who ran the story about you.

Once you have built your list, you are likely to find that not only are there more media than you can practically work with on an ongoing basis, but some media are more valuable to your business than others. At this point, it would make sense to prioritize your media list into tiers. Your top-tier media are those with which you must have ongoing working relationships. Limit the top tier to 10, with a maximum of 15 media. You want to be able to reach out to your top-tier media once or twice a month, and if you go beyond 15 media, that level of contact becomes impossible. If you don't make it to 10, don't worry. If you have none, however, you are probably not looking hard enough.

Your second-tier media are those that have a degree of influence on your target markets but are not considered the outlets of record for your customers or your partners. This is likely to be your largest tier. Finally, your third tier consists of those outlets that you will respond to when necessary and which have an interest in your company, but where it is unnecessary to do more than just respond. You don't want to lose any of these, but you do want to make sure that you have prioritized them, and by extension your response.

Regardless of who your priority media are, keep in mind that CCTV and Sohu do not automatically go to the top of your priority list. The majority of your opportunities with the media in China will be with print outlets or their online equivalents. Arguably, that is a good thing: print is the medium that is most conducive to delivering a powerful, nuanced, and convincing narrative, and the diversity of China's print media now offers opportunities to target progressively deeper niches.

Also, it is not uncommon to have your priorities change over time, and the media landscape evolves very quickly in China: it is worth reviewing your media list every quarter to make sure that you have your journalist priorities straight.

Once you have your list and your opportunities, it is time to start managing their requests for information. Some will just want background, facts, press releases, and photos, but others will want to speak to an executive about a story they are writing. Once you have checked your priorities and determined that the reporter is worth some executive time, you can either set up a live interview or, in order to be more timely, you can set up an e-mail interview or provide a quote for attribution.

What to do when a reporter calls

Whether or not you want to engage the Chinese media, if you are operating in China, chances are excellent that eventually Chinese journalists will reach out to you. You may not even have to wait till you get there: if your company is getting a lot of industry attention in your home market, it will only be a matter of time until some editor asks a reporter covering your industry's beat to find out what your company's plans are for China.

It is rarely much fun to have any reporter call you out of the blue: getting a call from a reporter from a Chinese news organization can be downright unnerving. The cultural differences, the language gap, and the gnawing suspicion that behind this call may be the hidden hand of the Party all combine to make you wish you didn't have to respond. It is tempting not to return the call.

Don't give in to that temptation. You have to respond. If a journalist calls and doesn't get a response, at the very least he or she will think that your company is disorganized and chaotic. At worst, it will be taken as a personal slight, and you'll have made an enemy who will gladly spend the rest of their career dipping their pen in poison every time they write about you and your company. But let's raise this above the level of personalities.

Keep in mind throughout all your interactions with Chinese reporters that they believe themselves to be the (and often are) proxies for their readers, and in some cases the Chinese people as a whole. Disrespect them, and you may well have flipped the bird to much of your potential market.

So when a reporter calls, try to have the call directed to a PR person immediately. If that fails, explain that you're in the middle of something, and need twenty to thirty minutes to complete what you are doing, and then you can talk, then reach out to your PR team to handle the call. First, make sure that whoever makes first contact with the reporter is someone who is not in a position to answer any questions about the company. This is where it gets helpful to have an experienced PR intermediary. Start by asking the reporter a series of questions designed to help you understand more about the story they're going to write, whether you want to be associated with that story, and, if you do, how you can be of help to the reporter while also ensuring that you and your company come out of this looking intelligent and China-wise. At the very least, you should ask the following:

1. **What is the subject of your story?:** Expect a basic, probably vague response to this. The reporter might volunteer more information, but usually only if the angle is going to be very positive for you.
2. **What is your angle?:** (That is, what sort of headline does the reporter envision the story having?) This question is good to

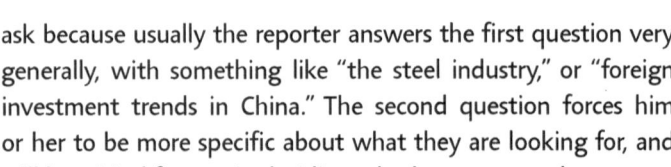
ask because usually the reporter answers the first question very generally, with something like "the steel industry," or "foreign investment trends in China." The second question forces him or her to be more specific about what they are looking for, and will be critical for you in deciding whether to respond.

3. **For which publication are you writing this?:** Many reporters, even those with a full-time job with a major publication, moonlight for other outlets. Journalism is not a pathway to riches in any country, and China is no exception. Many reporters (and a surprising number of editors) need second or third jobs in order to keep the lights on, and you want to know which publication you're getting.

4. **What is your deadline?:** This question all too often goes unasked, and for you it will be the most important.

5 **Can you send us a list of your questions so that I can make sure?:** This provides you with an opportunity to screen the call to ensure that you can not only answer the questions, but make sure that the answers you have ready are the best possible.

6. **We will try to get you an executive to speak to, but if our schedules do not match, would you agree to an e-mail interview?:** This is a great way to direct the inquiry to an approach that works well for everyone – the email interview – or clarify if a quote for attribution is in order.

The e-mail interview

An e-mail interview is a tactic that is common in China and rarely used in other parts of the world. An e-mail interview, in its simplest form, is when a reporter emails a list of questions for you or an executive in your company to answer, and usually attaches a deadline of a day or two.

There are profound advantages to this format. It allows for the delivery of polished answers to questions. The PR team and other executives (including corporate counsel) get a chance to chime in on responses. For the reporter, it saves the effort of transcription and allows for a speedier turnaround on stories. It allows the reporter to ask much more pointed questions, but it ensures that the executive will not be caught off guard. And in the case of busy executives, it is possible for others to "ghost-write" the answers (although they should ALWAYS be checked and edited by the individual being interviewed).

We like e-mail interviews so much that we use them whenever possible, but we also use care not to use them exclusively. Something happens in a face-to-face situation that does not occur via e-mail, and this creates the basis for trust between a journalist and an executive. That trust is probably more important in the context of Chinese culture than it is elsewhere. Nonetheless, given the constraints on executive time and the issue of deadlines, the e-mail interview will probably constitute the majority of interviews a company offers. If nothing else, it can be a follow-up or a precursor to a face-to-face opportunity.

Quotes for attribution

For a range of reasons, reporters in China find it extraordinarily difficult to get people to go "on the record" to be quoted in stories that they are writing. There are a number of reasons that executives give for not providing the media with quotes for attribution: fear of government reprisal; fear of being too high profile; and even a fear of being upbraided by HQ.

Consistently giving up easy opportunities to make yourself heard is, however, a mistake. There are immense advantages to having an executive quoted in a story that does not reflect poorly on the company. First, it positions the company and its executive as experts in the area in question. Second, it is an immense help in building worthwhile and friendly relationships with key reporters.

Finally, it gives executives an opportunity to hone interview skills in a more favorable situation.

A quote for attribution usually takes place when a reporter calls and asks either for a quote, or asks to speak to an executive briefly. If given a choice, take the former. As with the email interview, it gives the company a chance to deliver a brief and powerful statement that will be a huge help to the reporter, who only needs to copy and paste.

If the reporter absolutely must talk to the executive, and they are able to hold the conversation in a common language, request a list of questions and a callback in 20 minutes. During that time, the PR executive and the executive being interviewed can agree on approach, principles, messaging, and a few stories or anecdotes to include. During the call with the reporter, the PR executive should be listening on an extension if possible, and the interview should be recorded for future reference.

Working proactively with the Chinese media

At some point, perhaps early on in the process of building media relations, you will be able to shift the focus of interactions with the media from a purely reactive stance to a more poractive approach, either because of a story your company wants to tell, or because you want to begin building a stronger relationship with a reporter who is particularly critical to your company. One-to-one interviews are a common means of achieving the latter and of providing the kind of in-depth access to an executive that usually leads to a larger story (provided that there is news.) In some cases, a one-to-one interview is granted as a reward for a reporter who has done a particularly strong job in telling the company story, and in other cases as a precondition to writing a larger story. Either way, if you are doing this with one of your top-priority reporters, there is usually a respectable payoff for the effort.

Interviews and Chinese reporters

The phrase "one-to-one" is something of a misnomer: executives rarely walk into an interview without at least one handler and possibly an interpreter close by. Normally these are set up well in advance, often around company or industry events or milestones. They run anywhere from 30 to 90 minutes: 30 minutes when offered as a follow-up to a press conference or a speech, 60 for stand-alone questions and answers (Q&As), and 90 if the executive will be making a formal presentation at the start.

Keep in mind that the more senior the interviewee, the greater value the journalist and their editor will assign to the opportunity. For an interview unaccompanied by particular news, try to ensure that the spokesperson is very senior, if not the individual in charge of the China business overall. If coming in the wake of a major announcement, however, a department head or local person might work as well.

One thing we have done to great effect is to bring in area specialists for one-to-one briefings and Q&A sessions outside of the standard news cycle. This works especially well with trade publications and with other influencers that would benefit from a deep-dive into one or more aspects of your business. For trade publications, if you have a mid- to senior executive with area specialization who can offer insight into the industry as a whole, this can be a powerful means to cement relationships with key media.

Chinese reporters have their own habits in the interview, some of which would be considered irritating elsewhere. Nearly every reporter will record the interview so that he or she can focus on the flow of the Q&A rather than on getting all the facts down as notes. It is a good idea to have your own recording of the interview, so make sure you have a digital recorder (or phone) handy with adequate capacity and a full battery.

As reporters in China have grown in sophistication, some have picked up a range of tricks that may wind up catching you off guard. Watch out for these ploys in every interview situation.

Off the record: There is no such thing as "off the record" in China. Even in the case of a reporter who has no intention of burning you, it is a truism that a memorable piece of information is remembered long after the circumstances surrounding its disclosure have been forgotten, and will be passed on by the reporter eventually. It is safe to assume that everything is on record.

The deep background: This is another way of saying "off the record." All too often in China it simply means that you will be quoted, but there will be no attribution to you. Use extreme caution.

The non-embargo: The respected tradition of providing a reporter a story with the condition that it is not released until a given date is very new in China, and has often been more honored in the breach than in the observance. On one trip that we organized for reporters to South Africa, we provided a major product announcement on an embargo basis. Our mistake was providing it to three reporters. Each reporter, fearing that they were going to be "scooped" by the other, released it well before the embargo time, and we found ourselves talking to a very unhappy client an ocean away at a late hour. In an embargo situation, make sure you are working with a single reporter, make sure he or she knows this is an exclusive, and impress upon him or her *why* the news cannot be released before a given date and time.

The softball–hardball: Many reporters have become quite expert at softening up an executive they are interviewing with a series of very easy questions, often lasting half of the allocated time for the interview. Once the subject is relaxed and the chemistry in the room is good, the reporter will start an extremely uncomfortable line of questioning. This happens with print reporters, but it works with the biggest payoff to the reporters when a television camera is in the room. Always act as if the next question will be the killer, and you will not be taken by surprise.

The change-up: Occasionally a reporter will make an appointment to talk about a certain topic or set of questions that seems innocuous, and then once the interview has started launch into a separate line of questioning that is usually more intense and focused on an uncomfortable subject. A well-prepared and trained executive should be able to deflect the questions, but terminating the interview is not an appropriate response.

At the end of the interview, try to give a "last question" warning four to six minutes before the scheduled end of the meeting, and wrap it up promptly when the time limit runs out.

Small-group interviews

Often, particularly around major product announcements or the visit of a CEO, the demand for interviews will far outstrip the time that the executives have available to conduct them. In these situations, the small group interview works best. Something of a hybrid between a press conference and a one-to-one interview, these are a great way to have a more direct interaction with a group of journalists when there is something newsworthy to discuss, when time is constrained, or both. They are particularly effective in the case of visits of CEOs and other high-value executives who may only have an hour or two to give to PR during their entire trip.

Reporters should be informed in advance that this will be a group interview, and they should have an idea of how many other reporters will be there. Usually a group of 12–15 is the maximum size for an interview of this nature, but the smaller the group, the more mileage you will get out of it from each reporter. For this reason, it is probably better to have five top-priority reporters in the room than 15 second- or third-tier reporters.

Reporters are usually asked to arrive 15–20 minutes in advance to register. There should be tea and other refreshments appropriate for the time of day, and, if possible, a light meal service. There should be place cards for each reporter in Chinese and the native language of the executive, both large enough to be read by the executive.

To start the program, a master of ceremonies (MC) should introduce the executive, and at the very least the executive should say a few words, and if possible make a brief presentation. The MC should then take questions from the floor, one reporter at a time.

At this point you are likely to discover a disconcerting habit of Chinese reporters in small-group interview and press conference situations: the compound question. Called upon to ask one question, reporters will ask two, three, and even four at a time, which winds up monopolizing five minutes or more. You can try to limit these, but don't expect much success. It is better to factor in timing so that everyone gets a go: figure four minutes for each reporter as a working number.

Always provide a "last question" warning four to six minutes in advance of the end of the program, and have the executive wrap up right on time. The reporters will likely try to buttonhole executives for last-minute questions afterward. This can turn into a full-on melée, so it is best to limit this by getting the executive out of the room after he or she has personally thanked each of the reporters.

The press conference

When you have a lot of information to get out in a short period of time and you have a wide swathe of the Chinese media deeply interested, the press conference is the right way to go. Logistically, press conferences are about 90% the same in China as they are elsewhere, but there are some key caveats about dynamics that are worth discussing:

- **If you are new to the market, don't take questions in a press conference, unless you're addressing a crisis:** There are several good reasons for this, but most important is that all it takes is one reporter who has discovered a handful of rumors about your company to spoil it. Use the press conference to disseminate information, and follow up with the reporters who want to ask questions in either e-mail interviews or one-to-one interviews at a later date.

- **Don't skimp on the production values:** You should plan on having greeters, a backdrop in front of the venue, a backdrop behind the speaker, and an audio–visual team, unless you are in a venue where those things are either impossible or inappropriate. Having 20 or more journalists sitting around informally with no formal program, no munchies, and no comfortable seating is a guaranteed way to make them pull up stakes and leave long before you finish, and even before you start.

- **Rehearse, rehearse, rehearse:** When you are doing demonstrations, especially of technology, you would expect to make a fetish of rehearsal. But you should rehearse regardless. While each of the speakers may know the content, they need to get a feel for timing, flow, and technical preparations. The MC needs to think through transitions. Conducting a press conference in a bilingual environment opens the door for all kinds of hiccups. And nobody should be excused: certainly, a CEO's time in China is tight, but when you are spending a lot of time and money to put yourself in front a group of influencers who are critical to your business in China, you cannot cut corners. Either do it right, or do nothing at all.

- There will be times when a full dress rehearsal is impossible, such as when you have a senior dignitary involved in the process. That does not prevent you from rehearsing everyone else, and doing a full walk-through, using someone as a stand-in for the minister or ambassador.

• **Have a "green room" and use it well:** A VIP waiting room is usually part of a press-conference package. It is always nice to have some place for your special guests and speakers to chill before the event, and to decompress afterward. But if you want to really make the event work for you, do the following:

  • Before the press conference begins, make sure you formally introduce all of the VIPs and speakers. Not only is this a courtesy for guests that allows you to show the hospitality expected in Chinese culture, it also helps make the event flow more smoothly. You can tell when you have a podium of speakers who have never spent time together – the program naturally feels more disjointed.

• **Keep things tight:** there is a natural tendency to go long. Keep the whole program under an hour, and any presentation should be around 15–25 minutes at the most. Reporters seem to have latent attention deficit disorder (ADD) in China, and they have no compunctions about checking email on laptops, playing with their phones, or even falling asleep during such programs. Keep things moving quickly, and keep every moment filled with content and shot through with interesting insights.

Interpreters and press conferences

You should never hesitate to have a non-Chinese speaker participate in a press conference, as long as they are senior or insightful enough for people to listen to. What you MUST do in these cases is offer translation, an interpreter who can convey your thoughts in smooth, understandable Chinese. There are some critical points to keep in mind when using an interpreter in a press conference.

• Pick an interpreter that you have worked with before if possible. Not only will you be working with a known quantity, he or she will have more familiarity with the unique vocabulary of your company and your industry. What is more, he or she will have a feel for how your executive speaks.

- Pick a professional interpreter, not just a bilingual employee. Interpretation is a skill that demands deep experience, special education (most interpreters in China actually majored in interpretation at university level), and a precision command of both languages. Imprecise translations are worse than no translations, as critical nuance gets lost. For a press conference, professional interpretation is critical to a positive outcome.
- Provide any prepared remarks to the interpreter one to two days in advance. This gives the interpreter a feel for the program as well as an opportunity to look up any words or phrases that are unfamiliar.
- Most important – if at all possible – use simultaneous translation. Let me repeat that. *Use simultaneous translation.* Nothing slows down an event more quickly than the mind-numbing process of going back and forth from a speaker to a translator for an hour – it not only halves the amount of content you can deliver, but it makes for an excruciating experience for your media attendees, especially those who are bilingual.
- Double-check translations of presentations with a spare pair of eyes. Then do it again. Four or five checks is not a bad process – you want to make sure you catch everything.

Important aside: the decline of the press conference in China

Over the years we have lost much of our original enthusiasm for press conferences. Part of the reason is that they used to be conducted at the drop of the hat, as a substitute for good media relations rather than as a means of conducting them.

On the one hand, having 500 journalists all file stories that look like your press release within a day of your press conference gives you a huge bump in coverage and is great for your PR team and the agency, which gets to send you thick books of photos and clippings. On the other hand, coverage, while wide, tends to be uniform and banal.

What is less clear is the extent to which most of these circuses have any immediate effect on sales, or any lasting effect at all. The challenge with engaging 500 journalists is not that first story, but how you are going to use each of those contacts to your lasting advantage. How do you meaningfully follow up with 500 journalists?

There will always be occasions when the press conference is the right thing. News conferences are often necessary in crises, and when you are launching a major new product or initiative, they may be well worth the investment. But they need to be approached with great care and thoughtfulness.

For that reason, begin with the assumption that there is a better approach to your particular challenge than conducting a press conference. Explore a range of other options, including a combination of the approaches here. Only if there is no other way to accomplish your objectives should you consider a press conference in China.

Additional tips for working with the Chinese media

Beyond the above, there are a few final points that you should keep in mind when working with the Chinese media.

The unexpected

Even with pre-arranged opportunities that appear to be in the friendliest of circumstances, you have to be ready for the unexpected. All too often, a reporter will throw in a question revealing something about your company or the industry that you did not know, that you did not really want to know, or that you did not want known. Leaks, both real and manufactured, are discouragingly common in China. Be prepared for this, and ensure that you and the executive being interviewed have stock answers on tap for such situations. If you are aware of potential issues when you are going into a media interaction, make sure that you have stock responses ready. Answers like "I would be happy to pass you that information following the interview, but I don't have the details at hand" are acceptable. Remember: ensuring that the interaction stays on track is more important than an executive appearing to have all of the facts immediately available.

Bad press

Negative coverage of your company will happen, and even coverage that is either deeply flawed or outright wrong will appear in the media despite your best efforts. There are even some publications in greater China that have been known to make up stories out of whole cloth on slow news days. These will happen whether you engage with the media or not, and will sometimes happen right after you have had a meeting with the journalist in question. Keep in mind that, even in China, there is no way to control the media. They operate on their own logic, dictated by the business of attracting attention rather than some idealistic dedication to telling the truth. Preparation is the best way to minimize the chances of bad press.

Forget about killing that story

When bad press happens, do not bet on killing a story or getting a retraction. Story kills used to be a common tactic in China. They are far less so today. As noted above, media have forged a degree of independence in China that leaves them far less susceptible to pressure than in the past. In the case of foreign companies in particular, the effort to pressure a publication to kill or retract a story in itself becomes a story. The damage to your reputation can be permanent.

Getting a publication to print a correction is similarly difficult in China, and offers an awful return on investment. Dozens of man-hours are required to get a tiny box at the bottom of page 9 in some tabloid apologizing for a factual error, and it is unlikely to be noticed. Once bad information is out, you cannot simply pull it back in. The key is to prepare in the ways we have outlined below. Beyond that, the best approach to a slice of bad press is a loaf of good press. That offers a far higher return on investment.

Preparation means never saying you're sorry

In "What to do when a reporter calls" above, we stressed the importance of buying yourself time to prepare before engaging with the media. This should be a minimum of five minutes but don't spend more than a half an hour preparing for an executive's media interaction. Once you go beyond 30 minutes, the briefing starts losing effectiveness. During the preparation time, check with any other executives or departments that might be able to offer information or insight: nothing is more regrettable than a media interaction that could have used information sitting in an office down the hall.

Always have an agenda

Finally, make sure you know what you want to accomplish in a given situation before saying yes to an interaction. Go into each interaction with messages and a focus that will allow you to get at least as much out of the interaction as the reporter does. And keep your goals in mind. If there is no upside – or the downside exceeds the upside – it is entirely acceptable to decline an opportunity.

Working with the foreign media

The role of the foreign correspondent in China's ongoing development should not be understated. Foreign correspondents break national stories of historic importance; they receive significant attention and global accolades for their work; and they set a higher standard for domestic journalists to follow, an important function when local journalists often lack their own role models in modern journalism.

Yet for all the credit we give correspondents for venturing to the world's news frontiers and telling important stories, business people, including most public relations professionals, ignore or forget the critical role that correspondents can play in shedding light on the business side of globalization, and on the achievements – as well as failures – of companies that have stepped boldly into new frontiers.

Nowhere is this oversight more severe than in China. The emergence of the PRC from a backward, isolated enigma to the world's factory floor and, eventually, to the world's largest market is a fascinating odyssey, but it is all the more so when viewed from the level of the enterprises that enabled it. That story is best told by people who are paid to view those enterprises with detachment but who also have a worldview that provides necessary context.

Given the importance of China to the fortunes of the world's enterprises, it is a shocking truism that collectively there is probably no group less accessible to the China correspondent than the leaders of Chinese and multinational companies. It is as though operating in China were shameful, or perhaps some company secret, even as annual reports boast of the growing importance of the Middle Kingdom to corporate bottom lines. We can talk about China in New York, companies seem to be saying, but we won't talk about it in China. This is an approach that is outdated, counterproductive, and that may well be robbing some of the world's best companies due credit for what are often great accomplishments in a notoriously challenging market.

The opportunity is substantial. The Ministry of Foreign Affairs, the body charged with accrediting non-Chinese journalists in the PRC, does not release official figures, but best estimates suggest that there are as many as 700 registered foreign correspondents in China at any given time, not including Hong Kong, Macau, or Taiwan. Over 200 countries are represented, but the largest cohorts hail from the United States, Korea, Japan, Germany, the United Kingdom, and India.

Whether they are correspondents or stringers, the vast majority of foreign media are clustered in Beijing and Shanghai, with a smattering spread throughout the country. They represent everything from prosaic specialty publications like Treehugger. com to the huge bureaus of the *Financial Times*, the *Wall Street Journal,* and the global wire services. Many of the reporters are in China on short-term assignment and see China as a stop in their careers. Some fail to dig beyond the superficial, but a few, like James Fallows of *The Atlantic,* spend just a few months in China and manage to capture and convey its essence.

Still others, like CNN's recently retired Jaime Florcruz, make a career out of covering the China story and are expert in ferreting out the details of critical stories. Beijing has become a factory for superior journalism from foreign correspondents, with some, like the Beijing team of the *Wall Street Journal* winning Pulitzer prizes for their efforts, and others, like the *New York Times* and Bloomberg teams that uncovered corruption at the very top of the PRC government, finding themselves visa-less or jobless as a result of their hard-hitting coverage.

While the larger general news outlets receive the most attention, the majority of reporters in China are actually covering stories with a business angle. What these reporters find in China when they arrive is a story-rich environment that matches the growing hunger for China-related articles back home. Part of their remit is to speak to knowledgeable business people on the ground in China who can give them context and perspective.

This should be enticing to companies that are accustomed to lobbying these outlets for attention at home. But, as noted above, these companies rarely have the inclination or wherewithal to engage with foreign journalists. China may be story-rich for correspondents, but it is impoverished when it comes to business people who are ready to speak on the record.

There are several reasons to reach out to foreign correspondents in China as part of a wider public relations program:

- Foreign correspondents understand what you have accomplished. Better than their counterparts covering your company in your home market, the foreign correspondent can put into context the progress you have made in China and underscore that while it may seem middling from afar, it is considerable given the challenges in the market.
- Foreign correspondents are often more accessible. Getting a chance to talk to the *Wall Street Journal*, Bloomberg, or the *Financial Times* might be difficult at home with everyone clamoring for attention. In China, however, the environment is more casual, less charged, and thus more conducive to building a constructive relationship with the media outlet than at home.
- Coverage from foreign correspondents is not just influential at home; it is influential in China. Stories about companies doing business in China that are published in the global media get picked up, translated, and published in the local media with great regularity, and considerable credibility is attached to the stories because of the perceived standards of the Western

outlets. As such, these stories do not just have an impact back home; they can magnify your stature in China as well.

Reaching out to foreign media requires some care and some foresight. A good way to begin is to acquire for your company a membership in the local foreign correspondents' club, (FCC). Associate memberships are usually open to companies and individuals not engaged in journalism, and there are always plenty of PR people in the room at meetings. These offer directories of foreign correspondents in many cases, and in all cases offer a chance to get to know the correspondents long before you have a need to reach out to them.

It also demands a bit of coordination internally. Many of the larger news outlets – the wire services, the major New York, London, and Continental dailies – have reporters assigned to the specific beat of one or a handful of companies. Those relationships in the home market are highly prized and painstakingly cultivated. The possibility of providing a story to a foreign correspondent in China that will upset the beat reporter back home is high. This does not mean, however, that it is necessary to give up one or the other; it simply means that both the home office and the China PR team need to coordinate closely when engaging with foreign media.

Naturally, a desire to avoid crossed wires is only one reason to coordinate with the home office. The nature of global news is such that reports coming out of China about a company's industry or business there can have significant impact on a company's stock, particularly when carried by Dow Jones, Bloomberg, or Reuters. Care has to be exercised for this reason alone.

Still, as noted above, these caveats are no reason to abandon working with the international media. On the contrary, they underscore that the potential rewards are high enough that the effort should be undertaken, but needs to be coordinated.

Whether you are reaching out to local Chinese media or to foreign correspondents, it is essential that you give these audiences due care and attention. At the same time, they are no longer the only audiences who can move the perceptual needle for your company. In Chapters 6 and 8, we will be talking about audiences that are slowly eating away at the importance of media in a company's PR mix. First, though, we need to spend some time looking at situations that can cause disruption in the effort to build a brand in China: corporate change, and crises.

4

Public Relations and Corporate Change in China

Up until now in the book, we have covered the fundamentals of day-to-day core public relations functions. Over the next two chapters, we are going to address the specific PR challenges implicit in corporate disruptions. In this chapter we will take on several types of corporate change and what approaches PR needs to take either to ensure their success or to mitigate their risks. In Chapter 5, we will look at the peculiarities of handling a crisis in China.

On the road to building your brand in China, there are instances when the evolution of the company can, if not handled correctly, disrupt that effort quite seriously. This change can take many forms, ranging from alterations in corporate structure, leadership, product offerings, or policy. There are some common approaches that can help mitigate the potentially negative effects of major corporate changes on your brand and reputation in China, and we will look at three different types of corporate change and the lessons from them as a means of deriving those guidelines. First, we will look at the challenges surrounding buying or merging with a local Chinese firm; then we will examine the challenges surrounding corporate downsizing in China; and finally, we will look at the challenges surrounding a change in corporate leadership.

PR and China mergers and acquisitions

More and more companies are choosing to enter China – or expand their presence in the market – through acquisitions. To a degree, the public relations challenges they face are similar to those they would encounter in other countries: regulatory scrutiny, competitor pushback, customer uncertainty, and public discomfort with foreigners acquiring local champions. Not surprisingly, there are differences in the nature of those challenges in China that are essential to understand, and perhaps the best way of going about this is to examine two cases where China's particular circumstances made the difference between success and failure, and where PR played a role in that process.

Case study: Carlyle and Xugong

In 2005, the Carlyle Group, one of the world's largest private equity firms, announced its intention to acquire an 85% stake in the Xugong Construction Machinery Group, a state-owned manufacturer of construction equipment based in Xuzhou, in China's prosperous Jiangsu province. Xugong, founded in 1989, was China's largest construction equipment manufacturer, and was growing rapidly on the back of China's construction boom, but had reached a stage of growth where it was going to need significantly more capital. China was in the midst of a spasm of construction of both housing and public infrastructure (including preparations for the Beijing Olympics and the Shanghai Special Olympics), and manufacturers could not produce construction equipment quickly enough.

The bid's announcement[1] set off an outbreak of economic nationalism. There was an outcry in the media against selling off key assets to foreign interests, particularly at what appeared to be a steep discount to actual value. The CEO of Xugong's competitor Sany engaged in a one-man campaign to block the sale, going so far as to make a bid that beat Carlyle's by 30%. Reacting to the outcry, Beijing obliquely chided Xugong in public, taking the company (and the local government entity that owned it, Xugong Science) to task for not having cleared the sale with Beijing first. Combined with the online buzz, this compelled the government to take a stand against the deal. It called a meeting, which included Xugong, its customers, suppliers, shareholders, and competitors, to address concerns about the deal, but pointedly excluded Carlyle and its representatives.

Apart from the emotion, the concerns expressed by all parties were understandable and predictable. As the nation's largest manufacturer of construction equipment, Xugong was considered by many Chinese to be best positioned to become a national champion to square off against global giants like Caterpillar and Kubota. Selling it to a foreign firm – especially a private equity house – would have made it essentially a foreign firm on Chinese soil, and left open the possibility that Carlyle would simply flip the company to Caterpillar, Komatsu, or Deere & Company, effectively eliminating a major Chinese player in a large industry. And given China's growing construction boom, Xugong's rising profits would be flowing abroad, and prices for equipment could well rise even higher.

Carlyle's response was to go back and re-craft the deal three times, each time for a smaller and smaller stake of the company, eventually falling to 45%. This was to no avail. Beijing declared construction equipment manufacturing to be one of China's seven "strategic industries,"[2] and after three years of lobbying, Carlyle and Xugong were clear that the government would not sanction the deal. The parties walked away.[3]

Lessons: Carlyle and Xugong

No single factor put paid to Carlyle's bid for Xugong, and we lack much visibility into what happened behind closed does around the deal. Yet even from the outside, it is clear that failures in public relations contributed significantly to the decision by regulators to withhold approval for the deal:

- Public comments from Beijing make it clear that neither Xugong, the Xuzhou government, nor Carlyle or its agents, acting separately or together, ensured that the authorities in Beijing were adequately informed about the sale, and that were they were not consulted sufficiently early on in the process,
    - This suggests that Carlyle relied overmuch on Xugong itself to do the necessary outreach.
- Carlyle's case for purchase, a case that would have made clear how China, the industry, the province, and the city would benefit, was never adequately communicated to the Chinese media, and by extension to any parties not directly involved in the discussions.
    - It is possible, therefore, that Carlyle did not adequately make that case privately to other audiences as well.
- Carlyle apparently got the Department of Commerce involved,[4] and an Undersecretary of Commerce who came to Beijing to discuss the matter effectively accused the Chinese government of protectionism for blocking the deal,[5] which arguably assured that there would be no way out of the impasse.
- Carlyle allowed other parties – including Xugong competitors – to set the terms of the public discussion about the acquisition.

None of this is to suggest that Carlyle did not have a PR plan, nor that it did not conduct PR. It does make clear, however, that the effort was inadequate. It is likely that Carlyle, a company used to working outside of the public eye, felt that discretion was the best way to pursue the deal. The largest lesson from the failed Xugong deal, then, is that public debate can and will drive policy in China, and that the company that does not attempt to take a lead in that debate – either directly or indirectly – will find is business options foreclosed. Further, if you are not comfortable playing in the limelight in China, you must adjust your ambitions accordingly.

Case study: Coca-Cola and Huiyuan

Coming hard on the collapse of Carlyle's bid for Xugong but on the heels of Coca-Cola's triumphant sponsorship of the Beijing Olympics, Coke in September 2008 made an offer to purchase outright the China Huiyuan Juice Group for US$2.4 billion. The deal was Coke's largest overseas acquisition to date, and the company did not suffer from the institutional shyness that had apparently plagued Carlyle. Indeed, the Carlyle case taught a lesson that was not lost on Coke: executives from the soft-drink maker knew they faced an uphill fight for approval, and that public relations would play a key role in its success.

As a result, the firm reached out to a wide range of stakeholders, starting with the government but also including Huiyuan employees, their families, and their communities. It engaged in a multi-year image-burnishing campaign in advance of the acquisition, including sponsoring the Beijing Olympics and the Olympic Torch Relay. It sponsored exhaustive studies that demonstrated the key role Coke played in China, and the fact that it contributed nearly a half-million jobs to the Chinese economy.

In its efforts to court the stakeholders in the deal, Coke was blindsided by a new phenomenon: the public discussion made possible by social media. The company was publicly taken to task by ordinary Chinese who saw the deal less as a business proposition and more as the absorption of a rare successful domestic brand by a global colossus. There were even accusations that Coke was trying to quash online discussions against the deal,[6] accusations that Coke and Huiyuan emphatically denied.[7] When things looked like they were going awry, Coke reached for its checkbook and promised $2 billion in additional investment if the deal went through.

Despite Coke's[8] considerable effort, something spooked China's policy makers. Citing concerns about a monopoly in the juice and nectars business, the Ministry of Commerce nixed the deal, and Coke, like Carlyle, walked away empty-handed.[9]

Lessons: Coke and Huiyuan

There were likely several reasons that the government decided to reject the Coke acquisition of Huiyuan, some of which had little to do with the deal itself.[10] The claim of monopoly looks plausible, but in the end a 50% share of a niche market probably was less of a concern than other issues, many of which related back to how Coke addressed its public relations efforts in support of the deal:

- China had an implicit policy of restricting the foreign acquisition of a "large and successful" established Chinese Company.[11] If Coke did not know of that policy before it attempted to buy Huiyuan, there was a failure in research. If Coke did know, they failed to adequately address the policy through public affairs beforehand.
- Another implicit goal of Chinese policy is Beijing's desire to build strong local brands and turn them into international champions. Coke did not seem to adequately address this ambition.
- As the then Burson-Marsteller executive Will Moss noted in a post-deal review,[12] public sentiment ran high against the deal, and it was not helped when allegations surfaced that Coke or its agents were trying to quash online buzz against the acquisition.

Miscalculations on government support, on the value of a larger investment against China's loss of a precious local brand, and on the importance of public voices were, in the end, three of the most serious factors that ended the deal. And they were all PR-related.

We can draw several broadly applicable takeaways from these two cases: first, as is the case with most acquisitions, the primary audiences in both cases were the government, both at the provincial *and* the central level; second, public relations in support of acquisitions should not *only* focus on the government, but on other parties as well *including* the general public; and third, in all cases it is essential to address the primary concerns of the audience *as they are*, not as you *think* they are.

Guidelines for mergers and acquisitions PR in China

There are several additional lessons to be learned, which should inform how public relations teams in China – and their colleagues in home markets and elsewhere – develop PR plans around anticipated takeovers.

First, the government (national, provincial, and local) and the Party are the most important audiences in mergers and acquisitions (M&A) PR in China. While in other markets the primary focus may be a narrow group of securities and anti-monopoly regulators, the approach in China must be far broader. Chinese law requires government approval for most acquisitions that involve more than a few million US dollars. Up to a point, those approvals can come through local authorities. But if the acquisition involves a strategic industry, a highly competitive industry, or a high-profile foreign investor, you should expect the central government to get involved in the process. Further, if any form of opposition is raised to the acquisition from another province or municipality, you can expect the central government to take an interest.

Winning over government support is not impossible, but it is not simply a matter of the CEO showing up and taking the right meetings. As noted in the Introduction, China's regulators are no longer as favorably disposed to foreign direct investment as they once were, and local officials are more likely to be evaluated today on the basis of local gross domestic product (GDP) and job growth than they are on the amount of foreign investment taking place.

And, as we note in Chapter 2, it is necessary to know who the key government audiences are, how the wind is blowing in the policy environment, and to ensure that all of your supporters in government are lined up. However, the first key to winning government support is to win over local government. Since your acquisition is, in all likelihood, friendly, you can turn to the leadership of the acquired company to help make initial introductions.

Second, **you cannot get away with ignoring your competitors**. If you are making an acquisition in a crowded industry, one with significant promise, or one where you are likely to be seen as an unwanted interloper, you must be prepared to address competitive concerns from the start. Even if your acquisition represents no true competitive threat, if the acquisition is worthy of attention, someone will see it as such. Your challenger may be an SOE, a local private firm, or, in the case of foods and agriculture, a rural cooperative. The threatened party may actually see the acquisition as a threat, or they may want to portray it as such in order to leave an opportunity open for the future, or they may be a distressed enterprise that sees your move as an opportunity to call attention to their own plight, and use the acquisition as a means of currying support or a subsidy. If there is a way for someone in the industry to cast a negative spin on your acquisition to their own advantage, you can be assured that they will.

For this reason it is best to go into an acquisition prepared to publicly address those concerns, to do so with a convincing, fact-based case, and to mollify the government. Do not expect to mollify whoever is challenging your acquisition – even if they are protesting in good faith, the exigencies of "face" make a public climb-down unlikely – and, if possible, mollify those who genuinely perceive a threat. If you are moving into a crowded industry, or into one that is seen as particularly promising, you will need to address competitor concerns sooner rather than later.

Third, **consumers are influencers** in mergers and acquisitions. Whatever influence individuals not otherwise connected with a transaction once had, that influence is magnified by social media. While the government in China is nominally above needing public approval for specific policy actions, to consider local, provincial, and even the national government to be impervious to vocal public discontent would be a grave miscalculation. On the contrary, Beijing in particular has demonstrated increased sensitivity to public pressure, especially when popular sentiment runs squarely against foreign interests or large private enterprises. M&A public relations plans must include efforts to convince the public at large and address the opposition of private individuals when and where it can drive public debate.

Finally, an **understanding of government policy** around the foreign acquisition of Chinese companies and an appreciation of China's long-term industrial policy both have to be baked into the public relations plan and the plans of acquisition. These factors cannot be ignored out of hand – they must be addressed throughout the process, from choosing to acquire a company, selecting the target, and working through the acquisition itself. PR teams therefore need to be prepared to advise on these topics at any point at which they arise.

China and overseas mergers and acquisitions

As Beijing has become increasingly comfortable with its role in international regulation, the Chinese government no longer limits its scope of review to M&A involving Chinese companies. The government now sees its authority as extending over any companies seeking to merge if either company has at least RMB 10 billion in annual revenue (or RMB 2 billion in total Chinese turnover) and at least two of the firms involved have RMB 400 million or more in sales in China.[13] The sale of Motorola Solutions to Nokia Siemens Networks, the purchase of Nokia by Microsoft, and Glendora's merger with Xstrata are three recent examples of deals in which Beijing took an active interest.

There are likely several reasons why China has decided to take a view on these transactions, including a desire to demonstrate parity with the United States and the European Union (EU), a genuine wish to prevent the development of monopolies that might impact the Chinese economy, and an effort to prevent business concentrations that might inhibit the development of a global Chinese competitor. What this means is that companies fitting into this category that are considering a major merger or acquisition outside of China need to take a public relations approach with Chinese audiences similar to that they would undertake if they were purchasing a Chinese company. Not only do regulators need to be addressed, but also Chinese competitors, local governments where Chinese competitors are based, and the public at large.

If there are particular concerns in China's current policy environment, these need to be addressed as well. Are there issues between China and the home countries of the companies involved? Has the industry concerned been declared sensitive or restricted? Does the industry involved provide critical inputs to the Chinese economy? Are the companies in a new business, or in a sector that is evolving quickly and with a small number of players? What other policy concerns and developments might touch on the merger?

These questions make it clear that all companies falling even close to the RMB 10 billion/2 billion turnover rule and doing at least RMB 400 million in business in China should as a matter of course include their China PR advisors in the M&A planning process. Sensitivity to local trends and issues will play a key role in helping to address local concerns in a timely fashion.

Communicating downsizing in China

Much of what we are discussing works on the implicit assumption that your business is entering or expanding in China. Over the years, however, companies have found themselves facing significant downsizing or even withdrawal from the Chinese market, often for a range of reasons unrelated to China.

Decisions to downsize should not be taken lightly or undertaken
with too much alacrity. In at least a nominally communist country, the well-being of the Chinese employees
of foreign and foreign-invested enterprise is a
matter of profound concern among Chinese
officials. Downsizing without engaging
public relations in the process can turn a
difficult operational process into a
full-blown crisis that places a company squarely in regulators' cross-
hairs. The key is to make sure you
manage the exercise with empathy for
the challenges faced by your employees
(both those downsized and those who will
remain) and by the government officials who must bless the
procedure.

Once the nature and scope of the downsizing is laid out (which
offices or facilities, how many employees are affected), the
next step is developing a plan to mitigate the effects of the
downsizing on employees and on the local area. For employees,
companies are advised to consider going beyond the severance
compensation provided to employees under the law – do what
you have do, and then do a reasonable bit more. Further, provide
career counseling to departing employees, and hold job fairs
(inviting your competitors if need be) designed to give those
employees the best possible opportunity to land on their feet.

The rationale behind this is that you can almost expect some form
of protest from employees when the downsizing is announced.
Employees understand the political sensitivities around layoffs in
China, know that they have the ability (within limits) to protest
those layoffs, and realize that those sensitivities are particularly
acute in large cities. There will always be a handful in a crowd
who seek to exploit that political sensitivity, and you can expect

someone to have connections with the local media who will put that protest on the air.

Downsizing thus has the potential to disrupt your modus vivendi with the government, throw media light on your practices, and eat away at your goodwill among consumers and all of your other publics. For these reasons, the plan to mitigate employee departures should be designed both to be as fair as possible to the employees who are leaving, and be sufficiently generous (i.e. beyond what the law requires) to be recognized as genuinely caring about the departing employees.

Once you have put these actions in place, you can then shift focus to communications. There are three elements to communicating downsizing: the first is engaging stakeholders; the second is the announcement; and the third is addressing post-announcement reaction.

Stakeholder notification: Discussions with local government and possibly even provincial or national level authorities need to begin immediately. These should be handled by the most senior executives possible, with PR helping to provide talking points. In addition, there is a risk for leaks and rumors at this stage, so PR should be prepared to address these issues before stakeholder notifications begin. During this phase there may be some adjustments to the downsizing plan, and PR should be prepared to adjust to this as well.

Announcing the change: The announcement should always be made to internal audiences and stakeholders first. There is nothing worse than finding out that you are being downsized via the news media. An effort should be made to advise all personnel of the downsizings immediately, and for those laid off to be notified of their status within the coming hours or days. Once employees have been notified, a press release should be distributed in China, in the company's home country, and in all countries in which the company is listed on stock exchanges. The release should include as many details as possible about the care being taken to ensure a successful transition for employees.

Addressing reaction: Even when you have done everything to prepare, and even if you are offering an unprecedented severance package and guaranteed employment at other companies, chances are high that someone will feel slighted and seek to challenge the severance terms. Be prepared to address such challenges, which might also escalate to a meeting between the aggrieved and company leadership. The meeting should remain between those individuals and company leaders and should not be expanded to include media.

Throughout the process, it makes sense to keep your government interlocutors informed, and depending on the degree to which it captures media attention, it might also make sense to issue statements after meetings, or if there are follow-up actions. Plan on using social media to engage with outside audiences to the greatest extent possible – being highly responsive online will demonstrate the company's earnestness in addressing everyone's concerns.

The most important principle to remember throughout the process is the old saw about "leaving them laughing when you go." You cannot please everyone, but you will get credit (even if you don't hear about it) for making the best of a bad situation, for taking care of your people to the greatest extent possible, and for being transparent. If you are staying in the market, this will be essential. But if your downsizing is because you are withdrawing from the market, it will be just as important. The vicissitudes of the Chinese market are such that companies that leave for reasons unrelated to China often return when conditions elsewhere improve. You will want to do all that you can to ensure that you are remembered well and welcomed back, and that means making an investment in positive action and careful communications around change.

Handling leadership change in China

In the early years of a company's efforts in China, much of the reason for their success can often be attributed to the charisma, position, and relationships of the leaders of their PRC operations. While leadership is important everywhere – not just China – it is doubly important here. Personal relationships play a central role in trust-building between enterprises in China; people you work with often trust and admire your people first, your products second, and your brand third. For these reasons, a great – or even very good – leader has made the difference in China for companies like Intel, Microsoft, Motorola, J. Walter Thompson, and a host of others major global companies.

The problem, of course, is that executives leave. Leadership turnover is a constant challenge to PR teams everywhere in the world. When that happens in China, companies don't just lose a manager: they lose a critical part of their reputation.

The change management process begins with the deft handling of the former leader's departure. Even under the most acrimonious of circumstances, the company is best served by being gracious, even overly so. The "face" of the departed executive is at stake, and there is no reason to make enemies. Further, it is a loss of face for the company to hint that it had hired an incompetent, so keep departure notices positive about the departing executive, and about the future as well.

Ideally, you will have a permanent replacement in fairly short order, but in some cases it can take six months or more to bring in a new executive. The longer the time that passes between executives, the higher expectations you will face. Once a new executive is on board, the PR focus should be on getting him or her in front of all of your key audiences as quickly and effectively as possible

For this reason so-called "first hundred day" programs can be very effective in China. They get the new leader focused on a broad range of audiences early in the process, and they demonstrate to the outside audiences that the new leadership is focused on *them*. Further, they serve as a subtle tutorial for the executive in how the company handles PR, as well as an orientation for the PR team on how the executive thinks and talks.

The process should be led by the public relations team, but coordination with other departments is essential. The pressure will be on from the operational side of the business to monopolize the executive's time focusing on sales and on operational improvement. Be generous about sharing time, but resist the effort to continually push PR requirements out of the way. Make a clear case to everyone – especially the executive – on how *everyone's* goals are served by the PR effort of keeping the executive visible.

The beginning of the program should include an introduction to the public relations function in China. That introduction should coincide with a media training program. If the executive has recently been media-trained in China, the training should be limited to a briefing on the company's media contacts and a couple of scenarios to ensure that the executive is comfortable with company-related stories, messaging, and policies. Otherwise, the executive should undergo a full media training program that introduces the vagaries of Chinese media and provides practice with difficult questions.

The program should then include internal outreach. Full-team meetings ("town halls") should start at once and take place monthly. Regular written communications singling out and praising outstanding performers should be implemented early, but face time with internal teams needs to be the top priority. Getting in front of customers and prospects is next on the agenda – even if media are clamoring to get in front of the executive, customers take priority.

Armed with knowledge of the people inside the company and the customers, the next step must be the government. In addition to the most senior officials in each of the locations under the executive's responsibility, the executive should meet with all key regulatory agencies, ideally at the vice-ministerial level, or, failing that, with directors-general.

Once the employees, customers, and the government have been reached, it is the turn of the media. Under the best of circumstances the executive would meet with each of the most important 10–15 journalists covering the company, along with their editors, for getting-to-know-you meetings. While no stories should be expected to come out of these meetings (there really is no news but the executive), there may in fact be coverage, so preparation along the lines laid out in Chapter 3 should be undertaken.

The meetings should take place in an informal setting. Forewarn the executive that there will be interest in his or her background, family, and personal interests. He or she should be prepared to add this color in the discussions. Not only does it make the executive more human, it also makes the company more approachable. The media should provide questions in advance if asked, so make use of that opportunity.

Industry analysts (whom we will discuss at greater length in Chapter 8) can be a key source of influence on both journalists and customers. Choose two to three key industry analysts covering your sector and arrange meetings with them and the executive, usually in the office, to talk about his/her transition and their views on the industry.

Finally, once the rounds have been made with key audiences, the time has come to give the executive public opportunities to demonstrate that he or she has something valuable to say. In the first 100 days, make an effort to set up three to five major speaking engagements at industry conferences, or at conferences related to customer industries. Initially it will not be necessary for each of these to be "thought leadership" opportunities, but simply occasions to be visible, to become known, and to make it clear that the company is firmly on the industry map.

At the same time, if there are situations where the executive can start delivering relevant, thought-provoking insights, do not hesitate to build those initial engagements around areas that he or she is passionate about and can speak on with authority, and that are at least somewhat relevant to the company's business. Whether the speaking engagements are "thought leadership" material or not, at some point – perhaps toward the end of the first three months – the executive should plan on penning an guest editorial for a major business or industry publication that offers new insights, that is provocative, and that helps the company take a clear stand in the industry in China. The published article will serve as the capstone for the initial 100 days program as well as the starting point for the next stage, along with a social media program to allow the executive to engage directly with a full range of audiences.

As important as 100 days programs are, it is impossible to replicate the respect, relationships, and position of a longstanding and successful local general manager (GM) in a mere three months. Chinese warm to new faces slowly. Even when the new person comes to the table with a reputation of their own, that does not always transfer to the new position or the new company. The executive needs to be identified with the new company and new role even more strongly than with his or her former position.

For that reason, the standard first 100 days program should be viewed as a great start, the beginning of a process that could take a year or more. Once you've spent three months making introductions, it is time to move into a full executive communications program, and we'll talk about that in Chapter 7.

General guidelines for change PR in China

Every company, regardless of industry or vintage, undergoes change, and given the unique challenges of operating in China, it can often become routine. Through the examples above, it is possible to derive some core principles to guide PR's role in the change management effort.

Continuity is essential

Public relations practitioners in China should anticipate corporate change by being prepared to address it while ensuring continuity of all other public relations efforts in the face of change. It is a truism that a "business as usual" approach is essential in helping companies avoid market disruptions during the change process. Thus, the first principle of dealing with change is that it rests on the PR team to set the tone by demonstrating continuity in campaigns even while dealing with change.

PR needs to be involved early in the process, and at a high level: As the above demonstrates, corporate change in an issues-rich environment like China is at least as much a public relations problem as it is an operational, finance, or personnel problem. For that reason alone, the company's senior public relations practitioners need to be involved in the planning process as early as practicable, and if possible as early as the decision itself.

Overestimate audience size: The worst mistake you can make in conducting public relations around corporate change is failing to address one or more sets of stakeholders. A corollary to that is that stakeholders in corporate change define themselves. You do not decide who cares about your corporate change; the people who care do. You are more likely to run into a problem by underestimating the scope of the publics affected by corporate change than by overestimating them. Solid research in advance is essential to ensure that you are not blindsided, and when making a judgement call, err on the side of including more audiences than would seem to be necessary.

Keep it face-to-face: Keeping your audiences comfortable is the primary goal of public relations throughout the process of change. While it would be convenient if this could take place through emails, speeches, press releases, and editorials, experience suggests that communication should be face-to-face as much as possible. There is no substitute for the value of direct discussion – let the media coverage, the social media, and everything support that effort. not lead it.

Coordinate with HQ: Corporate change is precisely that – *corporate* change. Most of the changes discussed here, while China-specific, necessarily affect the entire corporation, particularly if China is an important market, an important source, or both. If you have a higher-level public relations team in the company outside of the China team, it is essential that they play a role in this process. Mergers and acquisitions will touch on the company's communications with financial markets; downsizing will also have financial implications, as well as possible challenges from international labor organizations. And leadership changes in China will be of interest to a wide range of audiences at home. All of these situations – and other instances of corporate change – must involve all levels of the PR effort. It is the responsibility of the China PR lead and the China market leadership to ensure that HQ does not steamroll the local team – a challenge we will discuss more in Chapter 7.

Properly handled, corporate change – even significant disruptions – need not disrupt business itself. The good news is that most corporate change is either expected or operates on a timeline that allows the public relations team to manage how it is addressed in the media.

However, there are accidents and incidents that affect the company suddenly, without warning, and with a severity that poses an existential threat to the company's business in China, and perhaps worldwide. This brings us into a realm that is painfully familiar to the public relations practitioner: crisis management.

5

Crisis Management in China

It feels like an ordinary morning. Traffic is heavy as you make your way to the office, and your mind is on the upcoming product launch and the 15 or 20 things that absolutely have to happen today. Your phone rings, and it is your boss.

"Did you watch the CCTV news last night?" she asks. You didn't.

"Neither did I," she admits, "but I got a call this morning from Bloomberg asking me to comment on why a group of Chinese rock stars are camped out in front of our Beijing offices and publicly smashing our newest internet televisions with hammers. I'm on my way over now."[1]

And then the question you dread.

"What should we do?"

* * *

It is no exaggeration to suggest that if you are a foreign company doing business in the PRC, there is always a crisis in the offing. It may be a crisis in the local PRC business, like GlaxoSmithKline

(GSK) experienced when the government accused it of nefarious practices among its pharmaceutical sales teams in China. It might be the sudden departure of your entire senior management team, a product quality scare, or sudden regulatory challenges. The crisis may not even come from China, as a group of US information technology companies experienced when revelations from the Snowden archive accused the companies of installing "backdoors" into their products that allowed the National Security Agency (NSA) to eavesdrop on their customers.[2]

Whatever the crisis and its source, how you handle the crisis will affect your sales, your relationships with your partners, and the degree to which the government is comfortable allowing you to continue to operate in China as you have. Handled poorly, it will damage your credibility with local publics, undermine or destroy your brand, and inflict lasting and possibly fatal damage to your business in China. Handled well, on the other hand, you can demonstrate to your publics that the crisis was a bad thing that happened to a good company, and lay the groundwork for a stronger brand in the long run.

The depth of your preparation and the deftness of your response to a crisis could determine the future of your company in China. Understanding this is easy: the challenge is drawing the time away from planning and executing campaigns, and dealing with ad hoc challenges and requests to prepare for the worst. But prepare you must.

In a crisis in China, companies can be – and often are – immediately overwhelmed by demands for information, the effort to ascertain what is happening, and the need to keep a range of audiences informed. Worse, to operate in China is to conduct business in an environment wherein blame for a crisis is not simply laid at the feet of a company, but often on government officials as well. For that reason, the minute a crisis breaks, you can expect to be besieged by a host of government officials at every level from a range of ministries, demanding to know what you are going to do to cover for them to ensure they are not sacked for letting this happen on "their" watch.

In addition to the government at all levels, local reporters, national media, foreign correspondents and wire services will all be calling for information, and if you cannot give it to them, they will go to others – including competitors – who can. Non-governmental agencies will also be calling you and talking to the media, and in some cases your industry association and your competitors will want to know what you are doing to make sure that all of this does not backfire on the entire industry.

We are going to spend the first part of this chapter framing how you should respond to a crisis in China. In the second part, we will discuss a more holistic approach to handling crises in China, which rises above the immediate exigencies of crisis management and will help ensure that a crisis in China will not put the existence of your business in danger.

Crisis response in China

NOTE: If you are experiencing a crisis right now, or you think you may be facing one, put this book down immediately and call a PR agency for help. The clock is already ticking and you probably only have a few hours – a day at most – to be prepared to handle what is coming. You do not have time to read this before setting the machinery in motion. Once you have an agency, have explained the problem, and they're gathering their people and heading for your office, you can take the time to read this.

If you do not have an agency with crisis management capabilities, get one. I would like for you to choose my agency, but if you have no idea where to start, any of the following ten agencies have teams with extensive crisis management experience and should have the capabilities you require. Pick one and get going.

Allison+Partners
APCO
Brunswick
Burson-Marsteller
Edelman Worldwide
Hill & Knowlton
Ketchum Newscan
Manning, Selvage & Lee
Ogilvy PR
Weber-Shandwick

If you are *not* experiencing a crisis right now, or you have a few minutes before your team arrives, we can take some time now to go through the key steps in crisis response in China.

Core principles of China crisis management

First, if you have experience with crisis management elsewhere, you will be glad to know that the fundamentals of crisis management are about 95% the same with crisis management fundamentals elsewhere. A crisis may last for hours, or it may go on for weeks, but how you act in the first 12 hours – indeed, in the first 90 minutes – after becoming aware of the problem will do much to determine how successfully you manage the crisis.

The characteristics of a crisis – as opposed to what we would call an "issue" – are that a crisis is usually a surprise and that it is characterized by a lack of sufficient information coming to decision makers. This information lag is particularly dangerous at the early stages of the crisis because *the company's leaders may not even realize* that a situation has escalated to a crisis stage until it is too late.

When the information does start to arrive, it becomes clear that events are escalating – or have escalated – out of control.

Coupled with the intense external scrutiny we noted above (including from government officials, who may be threatening to take control themselves or to shut your business down), the situation quickly devolves into a siege mentality, and, more often than not, panic.

Under such circumstances, the management response is often to heed the voices that tell you to shut off all the phones, ignore the outside world, and handle the crisis without distraction. This is an acute issue in China, where some managers will cite how "different" China is from elsewhere in order to justify a closed door approach. Rational voices will urge you to assemble all of the facts first. They will explain that admitting that there is a crisis will cause panic in the public or among government agencies. They will cite the lack of a senior corporate spokesperson able to talk to the media, *especially* when the CEO or GM are away. The legal team will be worried that any meaningful statement or response will be an admission of liability that can be used against the company later. Others will fear talking because it will reveal proprietary information, or the fact that you do not yet know how to solve the crisis.

Ignore these voices.

Word will get out. It is only a matter of when. And the more it comes from other sources – and not you – the more you lose control of the situation and, equally important, the quicker your credibility, your brand, your reputation, and the trust that your customers, the government and all of your other stakeholders have put in you will evaporate. It takes years to build a brand in China, and mere moments incommunicado in a crisis to destroy it.[3]

From the beginning and throughout the crisis, you need to demonstrate five key traits. (I apologize in advance for the cloying alliteration, but it has proven to be a helpful mnemonic device, so I will let it stand.)

Clarity: Do not try to hide behind words or hedge meanings. In all communications, use simple language to make sure your meaning is clear. This makes it plain that you are being transparent and not trying to hide anything or dodge responsibility.

Control: Demonstrate that to the extent possible you as a company are at least in control of the crisis response, even if you are not in control of the crisis itself and information is still coming in. Make it clear that you are working from set processes. Have responses ready that are clear and simple. Have the most senior executive available serve as a spokesperson.

Concern: Your first thoughts and primary focus throughout the crisis should be on mitigating the negative effects on the people, property, institutions, and environment affected by the crisis. Apologies to shareholders: concerns about the business are secondary, if not tertiary, particularly in how you address the crisis and how you communicate about it.

Confidence: Make clear in all of your words and actions that you are confident that you are going to be able to bring the crisis under control, find and address what caused it, ensure that it won't happen again, and take care of everyone affected as a result.

Competence: Avoid looking like an unorganized rabble. Know who is in charge of your crisis response. Get your information right. When you go on TV, make sure you get the interviewer's name correct. And most important, ensure that the company is speaking with a single voice and that information is flowing smoothly within your organization. Nothing undermines belief in your competence faster than blatant evidence that your company's left hand doesn't know what the right hand is doing.

Tactical crisis response in China: the first 90 minutes

To make all of this happen, you need to take some immediate steps as soon as you suspect that the issue you are facing is an actual crisis. First, you need to notify your management team. It always seems like at least one senior executive – if not more – are out of touch or on a plane someplace when a crisis happens. Everyone on your notification list needs to be alerted. If you don't have a notification list, you should make sure that the China CEO and all of his or her direct reports are notified immediately, as well as the global marketing and PR leads. This is the point at which you contact your agency and get them activated, monitoring the media, monitoring social media, and helping to take calls.

Next, a crisis team needs to be isolated so that each member of the team can dedicate 100% of his or her time to handling the crisis. Ideally, this team would consist of the most senior executive present, the public relations lead, the chief counsel, and whatever other executives are necessary given the exact nature of the crisis (HR if employees are affected, operations staff if it is an operational issue, quality control and customer service if it is a product issue, etc.). Bring some senior advisors from your agency into the team as well – as outside experts with no internal political agenda they will be useful in getting things moving.

Once a team is in place, you need to prepare a statement to be provided to all media and analysts that contact the company looking for information, and given directly to any media that have already run stories. The statement should be brief and to the point, making clear that the company is aware of the situation, is collecting more information, and will provide more as it becomes available. It should underscore that the company's primary concern goes out to those affected, and that the company is doing everything in its power to ensure that effects of the crisis on people and the environment are minimized.

If HQ and senior management have not been advised by this point, they should be, and they should be given 30 minutes to review the statement and provide any input. Regardless of the time of day or night at HQ, resist efforts to hold off on a statement until a more "civilized" hour. You are operating on China time, and the statement needs to get out.

By the time you have completed all of the above steps, you should be no more than 90 minutes into the crisis. *That* is how fast you need to be moving. The agency can distribute the initial statement to the media lists. Get it posted online and the agency can also get it onto social media for you.

Preparing for extended crisis management

Once the initial statement is out, take the time to divide up the workload among the crisis team. If this is an operational issue (a factory fire, an oil well blowout, a work stoppage, etc.), chances are that the senior leaders are going to be pulled back and forth between managing the operational crisis and communicating with the outside world. There is no substitute for the boss going in front of the media or speaking to the government. If you have two teams working on the crisis (operations and PR), keep them close – if not in the same room, in adjoining rooms.

Set up a hotline for crisis information. Ideally this would be a separate phone line reserved for this use only, which is set to ring a series of extensions that are staffed by people who can take messages or pass statements to the media. At the very least they should be internal lines that the receptionist knows are staffed for the purpose. Keep in mind that while the calls have to be answered, the senior people cannot come to the phone for each call. Help them decide who to speak to, and who to call back.

A senior spokesperson for the media needs to be selected as soon as possible. While it is always best for that individual to be as senior as possible, it is best to have the most senior Chinese executive who is media-trained to serve as a spokesperson to the Chinese media. This is also the point at which you circulate an email to all of your employees that includes the statement and reminds them that they are not to talk to the media or to anyone outside of the company about the matter until they are notified otherwise.

Sit down at this point and think through the crisis. What is the real problem (the crisis might just be the symptom). What is the impact of the problem and solving it in both the short term and the long term? Does it make sense to take decisive actions now that may be costly at the moment but are the right thing to do? Assume a "worst-case" position when running through this exercise. If you do not have all the information (and chances are that you will not by this point), you must work from assuming the worst and start working to make it better.

When you send your spokesperson to speak with the media, you should make sure that he or she is prepared to answer some of the inevitable questions:

- What went wrong?
- Why did it go wrong?
- Who is to blame? Is this your fault?
- What is happening now?
- What about your employees on site?
- What about the people injured?
- What about the environment?
- What are you doing to ensure that this won't happen again? Could it happen right now in another of your facilities?

Be prepared for the media and other stakeholders to get the story wrong. After all, they are working with less information than you, and the media in particular are on a deadline. Lacking any other facts, they will go with whatever they can cobble together from outside sources, social media, and their own information. Articles will appear giving information you did not know yourself, or information you did not want known. However, it is more likely that what comes out will be speculative, wrong, exaggerated, and spiteful. This is typical for a crisis. Do not agonize over it – simply see it as a signal that the more and better information you can get out, the less likely it is that these stories will keep emerging.

Your executives will be under pressure to keep stakeholders informed at every step of the process, and none will be more insistent (or even threatening) than the government. Keep all of your key stakeholders up to date, but get them on a schedule. Let your key government contacts know that you will be reaching out every 30–60 minutes. Set up a schedule for media updates to be circulated, and make sure that those updates are emailed to all of your stakeholders and internal audiences as well.

If you become overwhelmed by government calls, assign a liaison – or liaison team – to do nothing but take those calls. The team should not be made up of junior people or agency staff, but senior or mid-level Chinese executives who are company employees and who, if possible, know the government people in question.

It will not be long in a crisis before fatigue begins to set in, especially if executives get into a rhythm of dealing with the crisis by day and conference calls with the home office at night or early in the mornings. Fatigue in a crisis situation is potentially very dangerous – all it takes is one off-hand comment about how you wish it was all over to turn the tide against you.[4] If it looks like the crisis is going to go beyond a few days, set up a "platoon" schedule so that no individual is on crisis duty for more than 12 hours at a stretch, and to be sure no more than 60 hours in a given week.

These fundamentals should get you on the right track for handling a crisis. Now let's talk about how to improve your chances in such situations.

A holistic approach to crisis in China

Public relations people in China like to quote the old aphorism that the character for "crisis" in China is made up of two parts, one meaning "danger," and the other meaning "opportunity." The problem with this quote is that it is too Pollyannish. A crisis in China is about 90% danger and 10% opportunity. A significant part of that danger comes from the failure of companies to put a crisis into the larger context.

In my experience, most crises that companies experience in China are avoidable. You cannot prevent a *force majeure* or put an end to the vagaries of Chinese politics that keep business uncertain. But every crisis is born in an *issue* that, if anticipated, can be addressed before it escalates into a crisis. This means seeing crisis management as the fourth step in a crisis program that includes anticipation, mitigation, preparation, management, and recovery. This is what I call the crisis planning process. Here is the way it typically works:

Anticipation: Pulling a team of executives together, use a little morbid imagination and brainstorm all of the things that could go wrong for the company. Don't filter. We are not looking for the likelihood that something will happen, just that it could (e.g. natural disasters, human error, sabotage, competitive disinformation, employee strike). If it has happened to someone else or there is a possibility, however remote, that it will happen to you, name it and frame out what it would look like in the worst case. We will call these "scenarios."

Mitigation: Then, for each of the scenarios, talk through what *more* the company could do to avoid or mitigate those crises than it is doing already. Build each of those steps into a plan to be implemented within 12 months, starting with the steps that are easiest to complete and that will yield the greatest gains. Set up monthly follow-up calls to review progress. PR will have several potential crises of its own, but it must also monitor for signs that other issues are emerging and keep the team appraised. This will often alter priorities on the steps that the team must take for mitigation.

Preparation: Crisis preparation, at the very least, should include crisis preparation training for all senior team members and potential spokespeople. The training should begin with the senior management team, and it is advisable that executives from outside of China participate as well if logistically possible. Then the training should be delivered to the management teams for each major company facility throughout China, and the training should be geared specifically to the challenges of each site.

Preparation does not stop with training, however. Crisis management training from the public relations side is critical, but there may be other areas in which crisis training is necessary. In the petroleum industry, for example, it is often a precondition of insurance that exploration and drilling teams have in place a risk management program including operational crisis management plans. Those plans come with their own training.

The creation of crisis plans and crisis manuals has fallen into disfavor, and often for good reason. Producing a 200-page tabbed manual and stuffing it into a ring binder that gathers dust until the crisis hits seems like a fruitless exercise. However, several companies have come up with approaches that address the value of such guidelines without going overboard. The approach I recommend is to go back to the scenarios prepared in the Anticipation and Mitigation stages, and for each one:

- Write out a simple definition of the scenario – maybe two to three sentences.

- Make a list of recommended steps to take immediately.
- Name the recommended spokespeople, including back-ups in case the individuals named are unavailable.
- List the key audiences and publics, and why/how they would be affected by the scenario, including specific names if possible.
- Draft a series of key messages, with the proviso that they might change based on the specific nature of the crisis.
- Draft a media holding statement with blanks to be filled in for specific details.
- Have a section with special guidance for audiences that might be involved in the crisis: suppliers, retailers, etc.
- Draft an initial Q&A for the scenario, laying out the ten nightmare questions you are likely to get from Chinese media.
- Make a list of recommended steps to take if the situation escalates further.

At the very least, each of these mini-plans should be sufficient to hold the team over until more help comes from global, or until the full crisis team is assembled and ready.

Once you have completed these plans for each scenario, you simply need to append a bulleted list of dos and don'ts (or the first half of this chapter), a phone and email list for key internal resources, and a phone and email list of key stakeholders. Now you have all that most companies would need in terms of preparation. Except, perhaps, you could give it a try.

Simulation: While crisis training conveys and tests the skills that leaders require to manage crises, and a plan provides a roadmap to handle those crises, the only way to know whether your team is actually ready is to take the plan out and give it a spin. Through a live, real-time crisis simulation, you are able to experience first-hand what it will be like to manage a crisis under realistic circumstances, including phone calls, stories from the media, and a constantly changing situation. Such exercises usually take four to eight hours, are facilitated by your public relations agency, and provide a grueling test of how ready everyone truly is.

It should come as no surprise that simulation turns out to be the most important part of the preparation process. It identifies shortcomings in the plan (or in people's understanding of it), and underscores what needs to change in order to make it work. And it compels everyone in the room to go through each of the scenarios and understand their role in crisis management in a way that no memo could ever accomplish. When working in China among cross-cultural teams, simulation is an absolute must.

This step also provides fodder for going back to the Anticipation and Mitigation steps and reworking some assumptions. Often in the course of a simulation companies will find that they were insufficiently imaginative in the earlier steps, and need to have another go to ensure that the company is ready for complex crises.

Management: This is the process of actually managing the crisis, discussed above.

Recovery: In golf and in baseball, one of the first things you learn is the value of "follow through." In China crisis management, follow through means thinking from the beginning about how to turn the crisis into a long-term win. Harold Burson, the eponymous founder of Burson-Marsteller, once noted when talking about the legendary Tylenol crisis from the 1980s that you should always "recognize the value of short-term sacrifice." Though he did not say so, what Harold was thinking about was recovery.

Simply managing your way through a crisis may save the company, but it may not leave much to save. Crisis planning should always stay focused on using the crisis as an opportunity to deepen trust with all of your key audiences, even if that means paying out more to remediate the consequences, publicly admitting blame even at the risk of additional liability, or inconveniencing distributors and retailers.

The other aspect of Recovery is recognizing that when a crisis is over and the world has moved on, the company still has much ahead of it to accomplish. The work of repairing the damaged brand and reputation begins after the effort of protecting it from harm has come to an end. And the process is long and arduous.

For this reason, following the end of the crisis, all public relations plans need to be re-examined, and ideally scrapped altogether. The company is now working from a new baseline, and continuing to behave as if the crisis did not happen, did not affect the way people think about the company, places the company's credibility at enduring risk. Instead, start the planning process anew and build new campaigns that address the new reality, and focus on making the best use of the crisis in the PR campaign.

Finally when the crisis is over, you need to do a hard post-mortem. Nobody else is likely to do it, so it rests on the China public relations team to talk through what worked, what didn't work, and how to improve things the next time around. Scenario plans must be altered to reflect the lessons learned. Otherwise, the company has failed in its final test: learning as much as possible from the crisis.

6

chapter

Social Media and Public Relations in China

Since 2009, social media have begun to displace both traditional media and the World Wide Web as the primary source of news and information for a growing number of Chinese, particularly young people. All of this means that even as traditional media continue to grow and thrive in China, the relative decline in their importance has begun,[1] particularly among people born after 1980 (the 八零后 *ba-ling hou,* or "Post-80s Generation"). Reaching and engaging these young people demands that companies make use of social media.

Unfortunately, engaging these young people on social media is not as easy as posting your Twitter and Facebook content in Chinese as well as English. Government controls over the internet services to which the average Chinese user has access, combined with the pretty consistent failure of the global internet giants to beat hungry local competition in China and a significantly different online culture means that social media in China are rather different than what we face in the rest of the world.

What is more, China's social media scene remains a moving picture. While Facebook and Twitter have essentially settled in as the leading services in most countries in the world, China's social media platforms are still going through the kind of evolution we saw in the United States in the days of MySpace and Friendster. In fact, this is so much the case that many companies find themselves building social media campaigns around three- to four-month time frames, after which they stop, re-evaluate everything, and then start anew with updated approaches and even new platforms.

As of this writing, Tencent's WeChat mobile social media service is the hot platform for engaging with Chinese audiences; a year ago it was microblogging site Sina Weibo, a service that combined the best of Twitter and the Facebook feed. Social media platforms that predated Weibo have either faded or are struggling. Renren, Kaixin001, and 51.com all once looked to be the leaders, but strong mobile strategies and constant updates and enhancements allowed the better-funded both Sina and Tencent to outpace them. Today, it looks like we have gone from three leaders to two, and now we are down to WeChat. And the evolution continues.

For these reasons among others, attempting to frame what a successful social media public relations program might look like for China is a fruitless exercise. What is more useful is to lay out some fundamentals of how best to approach social media as a public relations tool regardless of platform so as to allow you to build a relevant social media plan at any given time.

In most organizations, the first fundamental decision that needs to be made about social media is "who is in charge." As much as with any other medium, on social media a company needs to be speaking with a single voice, and that has come to mean in practice that social media need to be managed by a single function.

Do social media belong under public relations in China?

Since social media's emergence, marketers, advertisers, and public relations people in China have been focused on figuring out where and how social media fit into marketing plans. It was fairly obvious that this was where audiences and attention were going. What was unclear was what to do about it. And this discussion has dominated debates in China for six years.

Unfortunately, few companies have stopped to consider where social media belong in a company's organization. The specialists in each field have approached social media as another means of conducting their activities. Advertising people – both inside of companies and in agencies – see social media as a channel for advertising, or indeed as another form of advertising, or as a way of enhancing campaigns in traditional media.

Digital marketers approach social media as a means to drive hits to digital content elsewhere. Social media specialists believe – and want everyone else to believe – that social media are so different, unique, and technical that there is a special magic involved that only they can understand, and that it is best left to the experts.

Public relations, naturally, has a role to play in social media, but PR practitioners usually define that role too narrowly. China public relations teams tend to approach social media as a fast channel to reporters, or as a way to bypass journalists altogether. They are not wrong, but that vision falls well short of social media's promise in China.

Getting the most out of social media in China demands that we see it as a space where people, not brands, dominate the channel. Until or unless this happens, the key to winning in Chinese social media is to get other people talking about you and delivering your messages; and the more influence those people have on the behavior of others, the better.

With that in mind, social media belongs with the people on a team who are used to cultivating influencers over time; those who understand how to develop powerful messages and tell provocative stories; and, finally, those who know how to track opinion and respond rapidly and appropriately to a question, a challenge, an opportunity, or a crisis.

Who that team might be could vary from company to company, but if you have been with us since Chapter 1, you can probably see why social media do in fact belong in public relations – at least in China.

Social media: separate or integrated?

Because form is so important in determining function, we need to address one more organizational question about social media, and that is whether it should be hived off into a separate team within the public relations organization, or whether the capabilities should be integrated across the team.

The newness of social media and the lack of clarity on how to deal with it have compelled many companies to relegate digital communications and social media to a separate department. There is validity in this approach: to make them effective, and to develop the approaches that will turn them into business assets, social media are, initially, best left to practitioners who understand these media and the often-unwritten rules that govern them.

But as practitioners get to know these media, they quickly discover that they do not have distinct audiences, but are extremely interactive channels by which to reach current audiences. As we noted in Chapter 1, there are two ways of organizing PR: one is by channel, and the other by audience. For companies that face a single public – usually customers – building the PR team (and by extension, the marketing team) around channels makes great sense. You have individuals (or teams) that oversee traditional media, the internet, social media, events, and channel marketing.

But companies that face a single, homogenous audience are the exception rather than the rule in China. As such, capabilities to address them must be spread across the communications/PR team, and indeed across the enterprise. The dedicated digital communications teams need not be eliminated, but repurposed – charged with understanding emerging social media, establishing best practices for using them, and disseminating those practices across the wider team and throughout the enterprise.

If your company faces more than two audiences – and most companies do – then it makes sense for the social media capabilities to be integrated across the public relations team, rather than separated into distinct parts.

Putting social media to work in China

The largest issue in social media in China, however, is the way that companies and PR teams approach their use. At the moment, most companies are at what I would call "*China Social Media Level 1*," where companies focus on using social media as a means of *delivering content*. Most companies have become adept at using this approach and, truth be told, Chinese social media are well suited for the delivery of content. All were designed from the outset with integrated multimedia capabilities (unlike Twitter and Facebook), and when that fails, there are always links.

This has proven such a satisfactory approach that most companies go no further with their social media programs than the creation of an editorial calendar and the content to distribute via the channel. Unfortunately, this leaves out the two most promising aspects of using social media in China.

"China Social Media Level 2" focuses on conversations: This is the point at which companies become adept at using social media platforms to respond to – and learn from – audiences. Companies tend to hesitate at this stage because costs are higher (you need to pay people to monitor and respond on your behalf), much initial spadework has to be done to make it practical (you cannot simply turn a 24-year-old loose with your social media account to answer questions or respond to snarky comments as he or she sees fit), and it can be hard to discern a return on investment.

But companies that have made the effort have discovered that it pays off, particularly if they are able to strike the right tone in the discussion. The company that has done the most with turning social media into a conversation platform is probably mobile device maker Xiaomi. The company has built much of its loyal following on the way that it takes user feedback online, puts that feedback into action by integrating it into the product, and then *thanks* the user who provided the feedback for their input and explains what they did with it.

In so doing, Xiaomi has revealed a key insight about Chinese audiences. Chinese spend their lives making an effort to stand out from the crowd, and engaging with individuals online in a respectful way that demonstrates an appreciation for their input strikes a deep chord, and can be a key step in building loyalty.

You do not hear much about Xiaomi's concern about the return on investment for the staff they need to employ to engage in these online conversations. On the contrary, Xiaomi can essentially write that cost off to a combination of customer service and R&D.

As for the concern about letting a 24-year-old loose cannon run your social media presence, the issue is easily addressed with what we call a digital frequently asked questions (FAQ). Set up as an online document, this becomes a digital repository for all of the questions and challenges that have shown up online, and for each one there is at least one authorized response, or guidelines on how to respond. The digital FAQ usually starts out with a dozen or so questions but grows as we get new queries, suggest replies to the client, and obtain approval to use those replies.

What we have noticed as well is that after using the digital FAQ for a period of time, the people we assign to monitor our clients' social media accounts begin to suggest answers that are extraordinarily sharp and to the point but, more importantly, carry a tone that is more human and less corporate.

So while Level 2 demands more preparation and ongoing monitoring at a higher level, when properly used it can be an invaluable source of insight, a means of driving loyalty, a customer service channel, and an outsourced research and development platform.

"China Social Media Level 3" focuses on influencers: Social media in China have proven to be a happy home for a growing cadre of experts and online personalities who carry considerable influence among specific niches of consumers. Beginning in the bowels of China's massive bulletin board systems, these groups of amateur opinion leaders have gradually grown to become cottage-industries in their own right. There are quite literally hundreds of individuals in China who are experts in everything from automobiles to photography to travel to microbiology, and they make a career out of books, videos, television appearances, and endorsement deals.

It is not necessary to write a check in order to build the support of many of these opinion leaders. What is necessary is an effort to engage them, share their content and ideas, and gradually build a relationship with them as a brand. Over time, this not only gets them to return the favor and share your content; more importantly, it offers you an opportunity to engage with them before making a formal approach, i.e. you can evaluate them, their expertise, their personality, and their suitability to work with you. It also helps to determine whether they are committed to other brands, and allows you to find out whether they would see an approach as a violation of their morals, or as an endorsement of their status.

Once you have chosen your key opinion leaders, you are ready to move into more formal development, which we will cover in Chapter 8.

Social media and internal audiences: Up until this point we have focused on the value of social media as a means of reaching beyond the organization. One area that deserves mention – and that will be the subject of considerable attention in the coming years – is the use of social media as a means of engaging your employees in China.

Traditional channels of engaging employees – town halls, video conferences, and email – hold little appeal for younger workers, who prefer to use social media as a means to communicate. Unfortunately, so far most efforts to build internal social media platforms have failed for reasons ranging from poor design to half-hearted implementation.

The situation is unlikely to continue, and there are a dozen vendors both in China and elsewhere who are working on figuring out how to forge a truly compelling platform. In the meantime, as public relations teams take on a growing share of the internal communications portfolio in China, senior executives need to begin forging their own social media habits. Internal social media efforts can be powerful tools to streamline operations and to turn employees in scattered locations into a unified voice on behalf of the company. In order for that to happen, though, they need to see the upside of engaging in yet another social media platform. The more senior executives use it as a means of communications, the more employees will adapt their growing social media habit to work, and the more network effects will come into play in the company's favor.

In short, a company is making the fullest and best use of social media in China when they are using them as a means to engage employees, provide content to external audiences, build conversations with those audiences, and engage influencers who can speak on behalf of the company, its brand, and its products. The responsibility lies with public relations to help the company get there.

Content: going glocal

As noted above, companies that have created global social media plans discover that when they come to China, not only languages but messages, approaches, and platforms need to change. Global social media plans thus do not transition well into China.

That's the bad news. On the upside, however, there is still content that can make the leap across the divide, providing that it is properly localized.

- Links tend to be the most difficult as they usually point to content in a specific language. Only use them if you can translate the content around the links and point to something in Chinese. Except in the case of technical publications, you will only frustrate your audience if you send links in a foreign language.
- White Papers, journal articles, and other documents will travel only if translated.
- Photos will travel, but make sure that you provide accurately translated captions and credits.
- Infographics are a superb way to communicate challenging concepts. Make sure you translate all copy. Usually the easiest way to do this is to pass the source artwork (not the JPG or PDF) to your agency. Not only does the copy need to be translated, the flow of the infographic needs to be maintained, and nit-picky typographic choices get involved.

- GIFS should be handled the same way as photos. Make sure that there are no words that need to be translated.
- Videos usually travel well, but you should expect to have to translate them, either by providing subtitles or, in the case of high-priority videos, by dubbing. Either way, the work is likely to be less expensive if done in China. You will need to provide the source video and a scripted storyboard for translation. If you are going to be doing a series of videos, you will want to set up a channel on one or more of China's leading video sites, such as Youku, in order to keep the video available. YouTube is not accessible in China.

In addition, you should be on the lookout for content created in China that can be used overseas when subjected to the same treatment.

"Black" PR and social media

We have approached social media to this point as a means of complementing traditional media in the effort to build direct connections with audiences. Social media are also a conduit for some of the more nefarious practices in public relations in China, and it is important to explore those to ensure that your social media effort does not stray into territory that could backfire on the company.

Since the early days of social media, when the term referred to bloggers, people who posted on bulletin board systems (BBSs), and users of Weibo micro-blogs, a small cottage industry has emerged to attempt to undermine those media and turn them into unwitting conduits of online manipulation.

In a process known in the trade as "astroturfing," unscrupulous agencies would go online on behalf of their clients and create dozens, if not hundreds, of fake accounts in social media sites, and then use those accounts to post positive messages on the sites about their clients and the products they make. Other agencies would recruit actual users, and then pay them for each post they wrote on behalf of the client. Those practices became so common that in June of 2008 *BusinessWeek* characterized the effort somewhat hyperbolically as "a war against China's blogs."[1]

While these practices are acceptable to some companies, they are increasingly regarded as unethical by Chinese public relations practitioners. Recent crackdowns against the "black" PR firms (albeit for other practices, including posting outright disinformation about rival firms) have certainly helped slow the process, but have not stopped it.

Public relations managers should use caution when advised that these practices are "common" in China and that eschewing them will leave the company at a disadvantage. The attention of Chinese law enforcement has already fallen on two of China's largest dairies because they engaged in such practices. Any company that gets involved in this sort of thing is setting a time bomb that sooner or later will blow up in their face.

Social media, PR, and uncertainty

Next to newspaper editors, there is probably no group of people on the planet more confounded by the explosion of blogs, social networks, and (in China) BBSs than public relations professionals.

And little wonder. Our companies and our clients come to us looking for answers on how best to use social media. When we counsel patience, experimentation, and observation, not everyone is happy with the answers. Senior executives in China, regardless of provenance, are type-A, take-charge people who expect us to provide solutions that are as pat as the press releases and press conferences. When we do not deliver them, there is a temptation to turn to others for solutions, even if the promise is false.

In truth, public relations people – and marketers, for that matter – are still trying to work out how to make the best use of social media. We don't have a toolkit of time-honored techniques and practices to address what is going on in the way we do for advertising, direct marketing, media relations, crisis management, government affairs, or any of the dozen or more sub-crafts in the industry. All of this is as new to us as it is to everyone else, and while some agencies and companies are further along in finding answers than others, it is all still experimentation right now.

So the best agencies, the really smart ones, start with a set of principles that guide them in the process. They look at the specific challenges a client faces, they listen to the audience, and they start improvising. Great online PR – indeed any great PR in an age where participation increasingly trumps Big Media – is like jazz, not a symphony.

Our challenge as professionals in China is to make our managing directors and our clients understand that shortcuts will only wind up hurting the company in the long run.

Pocket card: dos and don'ts for PR and social media in China

- Do use social media, in whatever form is current, in every campaign.
- Don't try to replace media relations with social media – they are complementary, not competitive.
- Do experiment with social media, especially new services as they develop.
- Do use social media to distribute content, but don't stop there.

- Do use social media to engage in conversations, but don't stop there.
- Do use social media to engage key opinion leaders.
- Do experiment with social media as an internal communications tool.
- Don't assume that anyone has "figured out" social media in China; everyone is still experimenting, and the platforms are still evolving.
- Do use social media yourself, and get the senior people in the company to do so.
- Do get your CEO an account on WeChat and on Weibo. If nothing else, he or she will get a feeling for how important social media is in China.
- Don't pay agencies to take shortcuts on social media, either by astroturfing, undermining competitors, or buying up paying for bogus followers.
- Don't overpromise results on social media to your boss.
- Don't try to bring your global social media plans to China.
- Do bring your content to China, properly localized.

Conducting Effective PR in China

Because of the sheer size of China, the number of media out-lets, and the importance of social media in the country, China is perhaps the easiest market in the world to make a lot of noise for a little money. For a relatively modest investment in a media event, in the space of a day you can count on 20, 50, or even 100 articles being published about your company and what it plans to do in China. I managed one event, for a mobile phone manufacturer, that produced over 500 articles within a week.

Unfortunately, China is also the easiest market in the world to make a lot of noise without it hav-ing any appreciable impact on your business. Companies that garner fantastic coverage turn around a month or a quarter later and realize that the effect on sales of that one day of coverage was minimal.

The message is clear: even if you do so nowhere else in the world, in China you have to move beyond the quantity or even quality of coverage and start to frame public relations efforts that are designed to move the needle for the business. For the purposes of our discussion, to be effective, public relations in China must be:

- strategic, i.e. have a lasting and meaningful impact on the company that drives it forward towards its business goals;
- efficient, i.e. attain those goals at a reasonable cost in money and time;
- positive, i.e. do not sacrifice the interests of any stakeholders in order to be either strategic or efficient.

Effective PR thus not only gets you a higher return on your investment, it also fundamentally alters the kinds of activities you will undertake. It unleashes creativity and innovation in the public relations process, improves morale, and effectively positions PR at the table with senior decision makers.

There is a range of factors that go into creating an effective PR program in China. In this chapter we will examine several factors that apply to all companies, and one set that applies specifically to smaller firms.

What are strategic public relations in the China context?

There are two ways for public relations to be strategic. The first is in the degree to which the wants and needs of the company's stakeholders drive company behavior, i.e. public relations having a lasting impact on how the company sees itself. The second is in the degree to which the company is seen as responding to and addressing the needs of stakeholders through its actions and behaviors, i.e. public relations having a lasting impact on how stakeholders see the company. When those changes are aligned to drive the company toward its business goals, public relations is strategic.

It sounds deceptively simple. But when viewed in that context, suddenly a product launch event with 100 clippings seems unimportant, but a cover story in a leading newspaper profiling the CEO's work on making the company more China-focused might be worthwhile.

The pushback I get on this idea most often concerns sales. Aren't public relations that helps drive sales strategic? The answer is that it depends on what kind of sales. PR that drives sell-through during Chinese New Year is tactical, direct-support public relations, which drives a short-term result. It might have zero impact on the way people see the company, but it does help push sales.

The problem with such PR is not that it fails to produce results – naturally, it does. The problem is that for those results to be repeated, so must the PR effort. When you have to repeat the action to repeat the result, the PR is tactical. When you can conduct a PR activity once and sustain the result over time, PR is strategic.

What are efficient public relations in the China context?

Efficient public relations in China is not about spending less money per event or per press release for the same impact. Efficient public relations is PR effort that:

- causes corporate actions to deliver messages to an equal or greater degree than communications activity;
- causes others to deliver or echo your messages more than you have to yourself;
- causes audiences to engage the company in discussion rather than simply listen to messages;
- delivers a higher return on investment, measured per the company's requirements, than it would for a similar amount of money applied elsewhere.

What are positive public relations in the China context?

It is possible to conduct public relations that drives a company toward its goals and is an effective use of money but that damages stakeholders and Chinese society at large in the process. In 2010 one of China's two largest dairy companies was accused of having hired a public relations firm to place stories in state-owned media that linked the baby formula produced by a rival to early-onset puberty in infants.[1] The allegations were untrue, and the police began an investigation into BossePR, the company accused of conducting the campaign.

The campaign produced sufficient fear that Mengniu crippled a rival and possibly gained new business, doing so for less than it would have cost to run legitimate advertising campaigns to achieve the same result. The effort was strategic, efficient, and altogether negative for Chinese society and a host of stakeholders.

Public relations practitioners are not obliged to take a Hippocratic oath prior to taking on their first clients, but we do operate under an obligation to avoid doing harm. In China, with its developing legal context and often dodgy business ethics, it is essential for public relations practitioners to conduct ourselves ethically. Failing to do so turns our work into a social evil.

Ethical challenges to public relations in China

This is a good point to stop for a moment and approach a subject that must be addressed,[2] and that is ethics. Having established above that public relations must be effective, it is worth spending some time examining one of the key areas that is keeping PR from being as effective as it could be: corruption.

Corruption remains one of the largest issues facing companies that do business in China. Most people think of corruption in China as the effort by companies to exert influence on government officials and institutions via inappropriate transfer of money or value; or the effort by those officials to extract money or value from companies in return for special consideration. This is the sort of misbehavior that was the target of the US Foreign Corrupt Practices Act of 1977[3] and similar laws from Canada and the United Kingdom.[4]

Anyone familiar with business in China will agree that while this is the most important form of corruption that takes place in China, it is only a tiny part of the ethical minefield facing companies. Not covered, for example, are improper payments to companies, journalists, media, analysts, scientists, experts, and other interlocutors who are able to influence regulators and are willing to sell that influence to the highest bidder.

Public relations is not exempt from the ravages of this moral ambiguity. Corruption and ethical challenges have dogged the practice of public relations since its inception, and despite a recent scandal involving some enterprising editors and journalists at a top Chinese newspaper, the practices continue. Local public relations staff will insist that these are an essential part of the conduct of PR in China. As a senior manager or PR practitioner, you need to understand to what degree these practices are inevitable, to what degree they can (and must) be changed, and the potential danger they pose to your business, before you decide whether or not to "go with the flow."

There are a wide range of activities in the public relations industry in China that, while they would be considered unethical or illegal elsewhere, are accepted practices here. While in isolation they may not seem egregious, they create an atmosphere of permissiveness that undermines the effort by many public relations people, both Chinese and foreign, to move public relations out of the sewer and into the boardroom.

The most common of these practices involves the so-called "transportation fee" or "taxi fee" to reporters in return for their attendance at a press conference or the conduct of an interview. These fees usually start at RMB¥300 and can run as high as RMB¥3,000, and are usually provided in a red envelope, for which reporters are not required to provide receipts to offset the amount.

To be sure, reporters are underpaid, have a very narrow set of expenses they can claim (if any at all), and probably could not afford to pay the cab fare to come and report on your event without you providing it. But the fees have grown far beyond the cost of taxis. A dedicated government investigator or foreign journalist could frame these as payola, little more than your company paying for the coverage it is receiving. At a higher level, your company handing a reporter a red envelope undermines the nascent independence of Chinese media and, by making the journalists beholden to companies that they are supposed to be covering, erodes their credibility with the public. At the very least, that means setting yourself up for falling returns on investment for your PR efforts in the future.

Most seriously from your company's standpoint, though, the biggest problem with "transportation fees" is that they are a gateway offense, which, if tolerated, open the door for even greater abuses.

Paying PR firms a set fee based on the number of words published about your company, for example, invites another form of corruption. The most common practice in these cases is for the PR firm to split the fee with the reporters, essentially paying reporters to write reams of laudatory copy in return for cash. Even more troubling, either the reporters or the PR firms will often make an implicit agreement with your internal public relations team to kick back a cut of those fees.

Increasingly common is the practice of entertaining reporters at posh restaurants, plying them with expensive gifts, or taking them on junkets to exotic foreign destinations. (Note that these larks are different from genuine "familiarization" trips wherein the reporters are entertained, but only in the context of learning more about your company's business. The difference is in the content.)

Once down that route, it is a tiny step to your PR team paying reporters outright to write positive stories about your company. Once you start doing that, it is only a matter of time before a reporter comes to you and demands that you pay them to spike a negative story about your company, either in cash or by buying ads in their publication, for which the reporter takes a commission.

Finally, there is the step into "black PR," discussed in Chapter 6.

Addressing ethical challenges

Not all of these practices are followed by all PR people or companies in China. Indeed, the further you move down the list, the less common the practices. There are excellent and successful companies (and PR firms) who eschew these practices, even at the risk of losing a short-term advantage. But the ethically challenged practices are still common, and the transportation fees are pervasive.

Until they are stamped out or drastically reduced, they will not only foster more scandals, they will undermine the credibility of China's maturing news media in the eyes of the public. The government and the Party can afford neither. And therein lies a great danger for your business.

These practices have been implicitly tolerated for 20 years, but as is the case with the turkey on Christmas Eve, the fact that the axe did not fall yesterday is scant guarantee that you will not be dinner tomorrow. The company that permits these practices to fester, when it does not have to, places on its legal and reputational balance sheet a liability of incalculable size.

And that is precisely the point: it is not necessary to engage in these practices. The quiet efforts of a growing legion of PR practitioners, the professionalization of at least a part of China's massive press corps, and the emergence of other channels to influence key audiences have made it possible to discard the old mold and conduct a better form of public relations.

Except in a few extraordinary cases, that will not happen automatically. From your PR agency and even your own PR team you can expect pushback, even vigorous opposition, to the pursuit of better practices. They will claim that this is the way things are done in China, and that it is impossible to get good results any other way.

There are two responses to this: First, make clear that these practices will not be tolerated, and that engaging in them is a termination offense (and mean it – put it in writing). Then soften the blow. Let them know that you understand that this is a departure for them, but that times are changing and that the company wants to be a leader in improving PR in China. Note that when they pull this off, they will be leaders themselves. If that is not enough of an incentive, it may be time to reconsider your PR staffing arrangements.

If you have yet to hire PR people, or are in the process of augmenting your staff, make sure that you ask each candidate two important ethical questions:

1. How do you feel about transportation fees paid to reporters?
2. Do you think you could conduct a successful PR program if you were prohibited from paying transportation fees or any other form of payment to reporters?

Taken together, these two questions represent an ethical litmus test. For that reason alone, they must be asked.

You will undoubtedly have to frame your expectations of your PR team in the context of a higher ethical standard. But if you have operations in China, this issue will not be limited to PR, and should be addressed both separately to the PR team and as a part of the ethical guidelines to which all of your staff must adhere.

Measuring effectiveness

Invariably when we talk about effectiveness, the discussion comes round to the topic of measurement. Measurement is a sensitive subject in public relations in China, if for no other reason than there is no uniform or consistent measure of PR's effectiveness that is readily available in the PRC. This is the cause of no small insecurity in public relations firms, and it is a rare proposal indeed that gives measurement more than a passing mention.

For a long time it was common practice in China to measure PR via advertising-value-equivalence, or AVE. AVE is a simple formula: measure the column inches of a print story or the duration of a broadcast story, and based on posted ad rates, determine how much an advertisement of similar size or length would cost. Then multiply that by a figure (usually 3) to compensate for the greater credibility of news copy over advertising, and you have the value of PR.

AVE, fortunately, is being abandoned. While it sounds simple and workable, it heavily favored the PR firm. Ad rates rarely went by rate card and were often inflated; there was no factoring of the tone of the story or its position, and the multiplier was, in truth, completely random. It has, however, left the PR industry in China at square one for measurement.

There are three approaches to measuring public relations. The first is to take the Einstein approach and suggest that not everything that is valuable can be measured, and not everything that can be measured is valuable. This is pithy but ultimately unhelpful – with procurement departments getting involved in evaluating PR programs in China, measurement is necessary.

The second approach is qualitative research: hire an outside firm to conduct an audit at the beginning of a public relations campaign to determine how target audiences feel about a company, and then conduct a similar audit at the end of the campaign. This is a powerful tool to demonstrate the progress that a public relations campaign has made in driving perceptions. What it cannot do is tell whether the money spent was spent well, or whether the same result could have been achieved for half as much.

The third approach is to cast the burden back on the company and, by extension, the procurement team. There is a sound rationale for this: Many executives view public relations as a necessity, and believe that the value of PR can be intuited more readily than it can be quantified (hat tip to Dr. Einstein). At the same time, if a company needs to measure the ROI of PR, it should measure against the degree to which PR drove the company to its quantifiable objectives. With no established tools, that places the burden onto the company to forge measurements by which it can judge PR progress.

This is naturally a costly exercise, and any result is likely to be imperfect. What is more, it is likely to take constant adjustment for some time to come up with a measurement that genuinely reflects the value of PR for the company. Nonetheless, the effort is well worth it: the more that the company retains the wherewithal to measure the effectiveness of PR, the less it has to rely on agencies, for example, to do so. Agencies have traditionally been tasked with measurement, a practice akin to setting a fox to guard a henhouse.

With an objective measurement system based on the company's objectives and needs and tweaked to compensate for China's unique circumstances, companies get the best system possible for them.

Framing effective plans

Another critical aspect of ensuring effective PR is building plans that extend logically from a company's long-term business goals in China and its short-term business objectives. For that reason, the top half of an outline of an effective PR plan – one designed to align with business goals – would look something like this:

1. **Business goals:** What does the business seek to accomplish in China over the long term, i.e. the longest period of time addressed in the planning process (two years, three years, five years, etc.)?
2. **Business objectives:** During the period covered by the plan, what does the business seek to accomplish?
3. **PR goals:** What does PR need to do to drive the long-term business goals?
4. **PR objectives:** What does PR need to do to help the company reach the short-term business objective?
5. **Challenges:** What environmental, regulatory, competitive, foreign, internal, and external factors stand in our way?
6. **Opportunities:** What unique and favorable circumstances do we face in sales, as a brand and as a company?
7. **Insights:** What ideas have we encountered that clarify context and point to a specific strategic approach?
9. **Strategy:** What specific approach will PR use to drive the company to its objective in China? Keep in mind that there is one effort, and one strategy. A plan with multiple strategies will undermine effectiveness because it will divide effort.

Starting a plan with this sequence ensures a single, focused campaign that unifies the PR effort around business goals.

Local China plans vs. global plans

As noted in Chapter 1, too often public relations efforts are rendered less effective by making China public relations efforts either too beholden to global campaigns, or not sufficiently integrated with the global PR effort. There are essentially two schools of thought, the exceptionalists and the integrationists.

The exceptionalists believe that China is such a unique place that there is little a global PR plan can offer that would be of value to a China PR program. Exceptionalists believe that only home-grown plans, practices, messages, and approaches can ever be effective in China.

The integrationists believe that there are insufficient differences between China and the rest of the world to justify two different approaches to public relations. China is essentially no different than any other market, except in size and speed of development. China today is just like the United States in the 1970s, and most public relations approaches will work in China.

Unsurprisingly, experience suggests that neither school is entirely correct. The truth seems to lie somewhere in the middle, where effective public relations in China are the product of tried-and-tested global best practices, augmented by locally born, deeply relevant tactics and techniques. This is best called "Glocal PR."

The strength of this approach is that it is empirical: it does not accept or reject a practice based on its origin, but whether the darn thing actually works in China. There is no set formula that dictates how much of your PR plan needs to be local and how much of it needs to be global. The answer is rooted in the company, what it is selling, and the preferences of the company's most important audiences.

What is more, the mix evolves over time. Tools that are effective today (Weibo, journalist familiarization trips) may be replaced tomorrow by new tools (WeChat, virtual experiences). Some approaches will be local by necessity – see our discussion about social media in Chapter 6. Some will be global by necessity – see our discussion about ethics above, for example.

Similarly, engaging bloggers is less important in China because bloggers play a different role on the web in China than they do in much of the West. On the other hand, participants in BBSs, online forums, chat rooms, and Weibo are far more important in China than they are in the United States.

Sometimes it does come down to customers. If your company sells to people who share more in common with your other customers around the world than they do with their fellow Chinese, chances are your mix will skew more heavily to a global flavor. This often happens with business-to-business customers, but there are consumers who share more preferences and traits across borders than within them. Early adopters of technology are members of a global subculture, as are early adopters of luxury goods and consumers of "pinnacle" products like yachts, private airplanes, high-end real estate, and bespoke footwear.

The challenge in selling to these global early adopters and same-industry commercial buyers is the same: finding a global mix early, developing shared creative and story resources, making minor adjustments for each market, and executing simultaneously worldwide.

What happens after picking up the early adopters, though, is that in order to sustain effectiveness of the public relations effort, you have to localize your efforts more as you dive more deeply into the local

China population. Global approaches win the early adopters, but culturally specific, locally driven approaches drive the mass market.

The glocal PR team

This has profound implications for the division of labor between global and China public relations teams. Rather than fighting over who gets what degree of control over strategy, campaign design, and tactics, the answer is more nuanced. Companies or products that seek out early adopters will naturally gravitate toward an approach where the global PR team leads planning. The master plan and strategy are created at the global level, and the China teams localize that effort and oversee execution.

Companies that seek to penetrate deep into local markets, however, will pursue a more distributed PR planning approach. While the global PR team may set the overall tone and theme of a campaign, the strategy, messages, creative, and execution are all developed in-market, sharing as much with the global campaign as possible but focused more on local relevance than on global commonality. This is the stage at which considerable autonomy must be granted to local PR teams.

The challenge for those teams comes in trying to forge a shared view of what the company is attempting to accomplish worldwide. In order for "glocal PR" to be as effective as it can be, a company needs to ensure that its global and China PR teams work smoothly together and share a common worldview. This tends to come from face-to-face work wherein China teams spend time at HQ, and the global team spends time in China. This approach is remarkably effective at breaking down geographic silos and forging unity among teams, which are essential for the glocal approach.

Being the little guy in China

Throughout this book we have been operating on the assumption that your company (or your client) is large enough to have at its disposal the resources to run large, long, and expensive China campaigns. For the first three decades of China's reforming and opening, this would have been a safe assumption. Today, however, small and medium-sized businesses (SMBs) are entering China at an unprecedented pace and finding themselves having to create effective PR campaigns with the tiniest of budgets.

Public relations for SMBs in China are less focused on organized, expensive efforts than they are on a China-specific brand of guerrilla PR. Many of the key teachings throughout this book apply to SMBs and are essential learnings for embarking on a China PR effort. That said, there are essentially three key guiding factors that are specific to SMBs and should guide their practice in China.

Note: in addition to SMBs, these guidelines apply to what I would call quasi-SMBs – small, tenacious independent divisions of large enterprises that function as the equivalent of small businesses in China.

China SMB PR rule #1: earn attention; don't pay for it

Advertising in China is very costly and expensive to sustain, and it offers a low return on investment unless you have the wherewithal to spend tens of millions of dollars a year over a number of years. Advertising in China universally favors large enterprises and tends to place them in a stronger position. Even among the Fortune 500, though, there are companies that are finding advertising in China to be too dear.

SMBs are strongest when they tell their stories. Everyone has heard about how the big boys have made it: Chinese, like Americans, genuinely like to hear stories about how a smaller firm outwitted its larger competitors. The more you can tell these stories, the more attention you will earn in the media and in social media. So don't buy ads; tell stories that will engage people.

China SMB PR rule #2: don't be louder; be smarter

Focus closely on who you are trying to reach, how best to reach them, and what they expect of you. As you conduct public relations, keep in mind that five to ten stories told in the right places to the right media and in the right way will be far more powerful (and far more effective) than trying to be heard in 500 media, or even 50.

As you tell your stories, be informative, be insightful, and do not be afraid to make the point that you know something about China and about your market that even the large competitors do not.

China SMB PR rule #3: sustain the effort over time

The biggest mistake that SMBs make when they come to China is that they blow their entire budget on an initial event or a short-term effort; and before they have had an opportunity to build much momentum, they fade away.

Winning in China is not a matter of the size of your effort, but of its endurance. If you can stay deeply relevant and visible for an extended period of time, the impact that your PR efforts will make will be much higher than a single pop followed by utter silence.

This presupposes an important point: when you come to China, be prepared to sustain a PR effort over the long term. Again, because you are focused on PR rather than advertising, on earning attention rather than paying for it, your marginal costs for a longer campaign are comparatively small. Stick with it, and the returns will be high.

Executive communications in China

One of the most important aspects of sustained effective communications has to do with the visibility of your China leadership. Putting a China CEO on the stump tour with the right opportunities can enhance the value of all the other PR that you are doing.

We started our discussion about executive communications in Chapter 4, when we talked about handling a leadership turnover with a first 100 days program. Here we are going to discuss what happens at the end of that program, or what even long-established executives can do to become public relations assets for the company.

Getting an executive known in China can happen in a lot of ways, but the key is meaningful memorable engagement with the full scope of audiences. Whether it is for an executive who has been with the company for years, or one fresh off of a first 100 days campaign, the program should be organized in four steps.

Getting to know you: For a new executive, this is the first 100 days program. If an executive has been in place over six months, this step may be redundant. However, do not assume so. In China, many executives in high leadership positions go for months and even years without conducting any outreach. It may not have been a priority in the past; it might have been actively discouraged; the executive might have been too busy with operational issues; or, as is often the case in China, the executive may have been too shy or afraid of conducting such an effort. In that case, a modified first 100 days program is in order.

Touching base: There are influencers out there with whom the leader of a China business needs to retain touch over time. Throughout that executive's tenure in China, he or she should undertake an ongoing round-robin of meetings with 10–20 key influencers every six months. This amounts to one casual meeting over coffee every fortnight, a schedule that will hardly fill an executive calendar and that will at the same time do much to keep 10–20 very important people on side.

These influencers should be equally divided between high-value media (editors of media that are important and influential for the company); industry analysts based either in China or in Hong Kong; key opinion leaders relevant to the company; and academics who have an influence over the development of policy in the company's industry or the industries of the company customers.

Meetings are set up so that the executive goes in with a list of questions of his or her own, so the meeting is mostly informative. Companies that pursue this strategy normally report to me that executives find these meetings to be the most insightful and stimulating meetings on their schedules. Rare is the executive who does not appreciate the touching-base program.

Thought leader: This is the process by which a company leader begins to publicly address issues that are of deep and abiding concern to his or her audience, but about which the executive is also deeply passionate. This effort begins with an op/ed story conference that helps the executive find his or her voice in the China context. The executive selects three topic areas about which he/she is passionate and that have a link either to the company's business or the company's customers.

The PR team then helps the executive outline one document for each area, which lays out the most unique and insightful thinking that the executive has on the topic area. On occasion, the PR team or the agency has helped the executive frame his or her thinking in a way that is more insightful, but the thinking and the voice are entirely the executive's.

The three outlines together, unified by a single, overarching point of view, are what make up the executive's thought leadership platform. Based on this platform, the team can start securing opportunities to speak, write opinion pieces for high-profile newspapers in China and in Asia, and distribute the thinking over social media.

The platform will be honed over time with each new article and each new speech. At some point it might make sense to compile the three lines of thinking into a book to be published in China in Chinese. The book makes for a great calling card, and it demonstrates that the executive is more than just a caretaker – and that the company itself thinks beyond simply selling products or services.

Global stature: This is the next step in the process. At this point the executive has been in his or her role for nearly six months, and it is time to start exploring speaking opportunities that will bring global attention to the company's expansion in China. The goal here is to extend the thought leadership opportunities to two or three events per year that capture global attention, such as the Boao conference, APEC, or the World Economic Forum Asia Meetings.

Internal chief: This phase turns the executive's focus to within the company. In a series of face-to-face group meetings around the company, the executive captures thinking and ideas from the organization. The emphasis in these meetings is listening, and the groups should be no more than five people at a time. The task here is to ensure that the executive is programmed to speak to influencers from within the company, to encourage them, and to take away insights from the meetings, act on them, and follow up with the employees involved.

Effective PR in China is rooted in a host of factors – strong design, solid planning, ethical behavior, measurable ROI, a strong balance between local and global approaches, and a leader who leads the PR effort by being the China Chief Communications Officer.

There is one last factor that must be integrated, and that is ensuring that all of a company's audiences are addressed – an issue we will cover in Chapter 8.

8

360-Degree PR in China

The phrase "360-degree marketing" denotes an integrated approach to marketing wherein the customer is surrounded by company or product messages literally everywhere they look: on TV, out of the home, on their mobile devices, in their newspapers, at the point of sale, and any number of other places where a marketing message can be stuck. The concept is powerful, and it has driven the marketing profession for decades.

Marketers are necessarily focused on the customer, so think in terms of that customer. Public relations approaches 360 degrees from a different aspect: not the media that surround the customer, but the audiences that surround the company. As 360-degree PR practitioners, whether wearing our marketing hats or not, we need to think about the full range of audiences that influence, drive, and enable decisions.

These audiences are important, because they offer something of incredible value to the public relations effort. Following a few basic rules and some pretty standard procedures will get your name in the media in China. Indeed, there is probably no other large country in the world where getting media coverage is easier. Unfortunately, experience has proven that no number of newspaper stories that look strangely similar to your press release is likely to change the way people think about you, compel them to go out and buy your product, or erase the slurs that your local competitor is spreading about you.

Those things can only be accomplished when you get credible people and organizations that are unbeholden to you saying positive things about your company and your products, and, in the ideal situation, delivering your messages on your behalf. This is the case around the world as we move into a post mass-media era. It is all the more the case in China, where the media is subconsciously perceived as the propaganda arm of government and/or big business.

In Chapter 1, we talked about the process of mapping your audiences in China. Earlier in the book, we have had a chance to discuss how the government and the media are the two primary audiences addressed by public relations. In this chapter, we are going to address the unique challenges and opportunities represented by some of the specialized audiences that PR seeks to reach, yet which are frequently overlooked, and how to approach them effectively in a China context.

Industry analysts: influencing the influencers

The growing ranks of industry analysts in China present a major opportunity to public relations teams, and one that is too often overlooked. Beyond the reports that they write and distribute to their customers, industry analysts are called upon by two of your most important publics – customers and the media – to provide insights on the industry and how it is developing.

Properly briefed, industry analysts will often speak to customers about your company when meeting them, but more often will become conduits for your messages and your thinking about the industry as they integrate your thinking into their own. They are also critical sources of insights and quotes to media in an environment where too few others will provide insights to journalists.

The additional opportunity in speaking with them is that, unlike journalists, they see themselves as experts and enjoy demonstrating that expertise. For this reason, a meeting with an industry analyst can be a significant benefit not just for the analyst but for the PR team and for the executive meeting with him or her.

The best way to approach analysts is to offer a briefing. Ideally you want to conduct these briefings one-to-one, using the most senior operational executive available – preferably the China CEO. The briefing will usually last 30–45 minutes and will cover material that has been cleared for public release. Following the briefing it is a good idea to allow about 45 minutes for discussion and mutual questions and answers.

After a few of these briefings you will start to narrow down which of the analysts are of greatest interest, based on the insights they offer and the coverage and quotes they provide on behalf of the company. Give priority to the best of them, but make a point of checking in regularly with each one.

The care and feeding of opinion leaders

As noted in Chapter 6, key opinion leaders (KOLs) are an essential public because, like analysts, they carry your messages to your target audiences, often framing those messages as their own, through social media, media appearances, books, and articles. Opinion leaders are respected by audiences for two key reasons. The first, of course, is their expertise, and the second is for their ostensible independence.

For this reason, opinion leaders walk a fine line when working with companies. They may want to work with you, but they cannot be seen by a cynical public as having "sold out" to you. Similarly, if they do not believe in the company and/or the product, there is no way to get them to influence opinion on your behalf. Even if somehow you were to compromise them with huge wads of cash, you would lose whatever benefit you sought to gain by undermining their credibility.

What you seek to earn with KOLs is their *belief* in your company, in your product, and your brand. They can be won over with an emotional appeal, but only if they are able to make a rational case for your company that is plausible among their followers will you get the full benefit of working with them. For this reason, as you screen and select KOLs as partners, select those who are already believers.

As noted in Chapter 6, select a KOL to work with by engaging with them online and getting a feel for who they are and how they operate, along with their stance on your company and products. Once you have made your choice, the next stage is the most delicate: the approach.

The approach is best conducted in person, and then by the most senior executive possible. Usually a lunch meeting will work, accompanied by discussions about what the company seeks to accomplish. The atmosphere should be informal, but the meal should conclude with a formal offer to work with the company.

Every KOL is motivated by different factors, with the six most common being: a predisposition toward your company or your product (i.e. a fan); an ulterior motive, usually because working with you will raise his or her stature, provide a chance to write a book, or some such opportunity; money; ideology, meaning that he or she is motivated to work with you because your company represents something in which he or she believes quite deeply; curiosity, because he or she is interested to learn more about the company or just wants to know what it would be like to work with you; and ego, because working with you re-affirms his or her self-image. We use the mnemonic PUMICE: predisposition, ulterior motive, money, ideology, curiosity, ego.

Once you have worked out which approach is the best, it is always wise to sign an agreement that lays out the mutual obligations of the parties, including, if necessary, a non-disclosure agreement (if you are planning on introducing the KOL to proprietary information).

After he or she is signed up, a briefing is in order. In the case of some KOLs, it might be worth running them through a media training program to enhance their confidence and presentability.

KOLs with whom you have a written agreement should commit to a rough schedule of activities that they will conduct on your behalf – social media posts, television appearances, videos, articles, inclusions in books, etc. The team should not assume that the KOL will do all of this – it is important to follow up and have verification of the completion of each activity.

Every six months it is worth reviewing the role each KOL is playing, and ensure that they are not only living up to their word, but that you can see a visible impact from their activities. If not, consider working with them to up their game a bit.

The challenge with KOLs is that once you have engaged them it is difficult, indeed awkward, to terminate an arrangement, so make very sure that you want to work with a KOL before contracting him or her in the first place.

Every employee a spokesperson

Traditionally, public relations practitioners treat it as an article of faith that corporate spokespeople should be limited in number, very senior, media trained, and highly presentable. It is time that we admit that we no longer have the luxury of choosing corporate spokespeople: they now choose themselves.

The rise of social media means that in a typical company the majority of your employees – and possibly all of them – are online and in a position to talk about your company. For the PR professional, there are two likely reactions to this fact: the horror of realizing that this is in fact the case, or the apprehension of an unparalleled opportunity.

Control-freak PR people are very uncomfortable with the idea of employees tweeting and blogging about the company. They tend to advocate restrictive social media policies that discourage employees from talking at all about the company and its business on private social media accounts. There is nothing inherently wrong with this approach.

The problem is that control comes at the price of sacrificing the combined power of all those employees' voices speaking on behalf of the company, which can be highly beneficial especially if they have workable guidelines and some help with content every now and then. We may be struggling to recruit a single opinion leader, when in fact without realizing it we may already have one – or several – working under our own roof.

This is why there is such a strong case in favor of recruiting these folks to the cause. It is hard to measure the cumulative value of hundreds – if not thousands – of people fanning out across the internet and just saying good things about you, but it is certainly higher than zero, and the cost is negligible.

Making this happen involves the creation of a set of social media guidelines that spell out clearly and succinctly what company-related information is an absolute no-no, including proprietary information, financial information, and the like. It should also spell out all of the different types of company-related information that can be shared, along with a range of samples. Each employee should also be encouraged to share his or her social media presences with the company so that the company can follow them.

This not only empowers employees to engage on a company's behalf in perhaps thousands of conversations each year, but it allows them to start building social engagement with the company and each other, a critical precursor to developing internal social media networks that can enhance the company's operation.

Connecting with the academy

The fourth critical group that should not be ignored are the scholars, academics, and think-tank members across China. There are three kinds of academics (I'll use this term to include the other two) that you should be reaching out to as a part of your PR efforts. The first type is academics in your company's field who are in a position to encourage high-quality graduates to join your firm. Competition is intense in every field, but a well-placed word from a respected professor will put your company on the radar of some of China's best candidates.

The second type of academic is one who can influence the opinions of government officials about your company and its business, or endorse your importance to the country and the economy as a whole. These academics are always good to have in your back pocket for the day when the tide of government opinion turns against you. They should not be tapped just to go and speak to someone on your behalf, but should be held back until they are needed.

The third type of academic that will be important to you is one who takes a consultative role in developing and drafting laws and government policy that affect you or your industry. As China's legal system evolves, regulations are delving into increasingly technical fields that are beyond the ken of China's lawmakers. For this reason, those bodies are turning to experts in both the ministries and academia to assist in the drafting of regulation and legislation.

It is not hard to see how this third group would be of acute value. Not only would a company have an opportunity to provide its viewpoint, it might also benefit from understanding the point of view of the individuals drafting the regulation, and their understanding of the intent behind the law.

Reaching out to academics is a bit less straightforward than reaching out to industry analysts, but the approach is largely the same: it is an opportunity to exchange information and viewpoints that are of interest to both sides. As with the analysts, senior executives should be involved in the outreach to academics. Senior professors don't want to waste their time with junior staff or PR people – they want access to executives who have something to offer.

Once you have established initial contact and held a first meeting, ensure that you schedule regular updates every six months. At each meeting your executive should bring along something of interest. These relationships will pay considerable dividends, so it is well worth investing time and effort in them.

Reacting to activists

There are over a dozen major audiences that a company needs to engage with, but the last of the critical and often overlooked audiences are the activists. As noted, these are not the voices of political opposition, but the small legion of people in China who are deeply patriotic and very vocal about it. While not exactly xenophobic, they are no friends of foreign business, and can be roused to take strong stands against international companies.

Under normal circumstances, the proper approach to these individuals would be to ignore them so as not to legitimize their opinions or behavior. In China's evolving political environment, however, that may no longer be possible for a growing number of firms. It may therefore be necessary to reach out and engage with the more influential – and more balanced – of these legitimate activists.

The time to engage is when you can see the potential for a particularly vocal activist to take a stand against the company or its industry, but has not done so yet. Once an activist's position is set, it is unlikely to change. Before it is set, however, it is often open to some influence; hence you should arrange a meeting.

Initial outreach should be made by an experienced PR professional, and it should be away from the company offices. The initial meeting is a "getting to know you," and should be conducted on the basis of wanting to listen, but also wanting to share information. The approach should be handled with care and sensitivity. You do not want to appear to be seeking to influence: your goal should be to inform. Any attempt to push is unlikely to have a positive result.

Getting others to speak for you

A key role for public relations is the creation of a chorus of voices to speak on your behalf across a range of issues. The audiences above – in addition to the media, the government, and the public at large – collectively represent a powerful chorus who could either speak for you or against you.

Throughout your dealings with these audiences, it is imperative that all outreach and contact is above board. No company can afford to have a reputation of being up to something secret, and a foreign company even less so. To extend the metaphor, when building your chorus of voices, your job as choirmaster is to lay out a song that all can sing in good conscience. Only then will the influence be genuine, and the results what you seek.

9

Public Relations
Agencies in China

PR agencies got their start in China in 1980. That year, a small group of boutique "government relations" firms practicing a specialized form of public relations called "public affairs" opened their doors to help foreign firms try to navigate the labyrinths of Chinese government power. Throughout the 1980s, nothing moved for enterprise in China without the specific approval – and often the direct assistance – of senior government leaders. The key for hopeful international firms was to win the approval and help of a set of government officials: heads of state-owned enterprises; ministers or vice-ministers of relevant industrial ministries; or, indeed, the nation's highest leaders. Public affairs firms offered counsel to clients on whom to speak to, what to say, and how to frame their businesses to match what China would permit. They also provided introductions to senior leaders capable of opening doors.

As the government gradually became more comfortable dealing with foreign companies, managing government relationships became an established craft. Companies began conducting actual business in China, importing, making, and then selling things. It quickly became necessary to search out ways to reach potential customers in a country with no established marketing channels.

Following their clients, a handful of global public relations firms began setting up joint ventures, starting with Burson-Marsteller's groundbreaking joint venture with the Xinhua News Agency in 1986. The global firms started with public affairs but quickly branched into media relations, reaching out to what was then China's modest handful of party-controlled newspapers, magazines, and TV stations to gain coverage for their clients. PR firms organized some of China's earliest press conferences, contending with the delicate politics and protocol between foreign and local joint-venture partners and the government officials who felt obliged to attend. CEOs would land in Beijing, meet the President, converse with the media, attend a ribbon-cutting ceremony, and get photographed on the streets.

By the mid-1990s, there were over a dozen major PR firms and countless small boutiques, all augmenting the small but growing PR departments attached to joint ventures and to the representative offices of the global firms that were investing in China. There was a clear stratification among the agencies. The international firms offered a broad range of capabilities, experienced staff, and the assurance of consistently high-quality delivery. The local boutiques were scrappy ventures that were more narrowly focused and rather less experienced; however, compared with their foreign counterparts, they offered clients substantially lower costs and teams that were arguably more in tune with the Chinese media and people.

China boasts one of the largest selections of public relations agencies anywhere on the planet, with global firms, local agencies, and global hybrids of all sizes, each having a unique set of talents, capabilities, and specializations. This means that most companies are able to find a PR firm that matches their needs, both real and perceived.

China's PR agency landscape

The landscape of PR agencies in China is sufficiently varied that most companies are able to find a firm that matches their needs, both real and perceived. The agencies come in all shapes and sizes.

The global majors

The global majors are the small group of the world's largest public relations agencies. These firms brought PR to China back in the days when there was more risk than business, and helped to build the industry. Today, at least 40 of the 50 largest PR firms in the world (as estimated by the Holmes Report) have at least one office in China.

The advantage of working with the global majors is that with the scale comes access to a range of capabilities and the ability to meet whatever needs you might have. The disadvantage is that unless you are of a similar size to Microsoft, McDonalds, BMW, or Hewlett Packard, it is going to be difficult to get the attention of senior leaders on an ongoing basis. Service will always be satisfactory, but it will be more expensive, and while there is assurance in the size and names of these agencies, sophisticated customers will know that there are other options beyond the big names.

Global/international mid-sized firms

In addition to the global majors, there is now a large and increasingly professional crop of agencies that were started by local Chinese, many of them veterans of international firms. While a lot were originally independent, the majority of the founders have sold out to global majors and moved on.

The better of these firms boast a dedication to service and focus on a handful of specific industries in which they have developed deep competencies.

Local foreign firms

Local foreign firms are agencies that were started in China by non-Chinese. While usually fairly small in scale, they offer an unparalleled degree of high-quality personal service. These firms usually have limited resources, but are pleasant to work with, have deep competencies in two or three industries or specialty areas, and usually emphasize strategic assistance rather than simple execution.

The Chinese majors

These firms are local agencies that have managed to remain independent as they have grown to a scale large enough to match the global majors in size. Blue Focus is the leading example of this kind of firm, one that focuses on scale to service the largest clients. Most of these firms still operate on a basic level of service consistently applied: their stock-in-trade is unparalleled efficiency in execution.

Local mid-sized firms

Local mid-sized firms usually offer excellent value for the dollar, strong experience, and a decent level of supervision by senior Chinese leadership. Like the Chinese majors, these firms usually excel in efficient execution.

Local small firms

As with their larger brethren, the local small firms usually focus on efficient execution. While their size ensures that there are fewer resources, the direct attention from founders and senior practitioners can make these firms a better bet for small companies just sneaking into the market.

Why, when, and how to hire a PR agency

One of the first decisions any company faces when building its PR presence in China is whether to create a full, robust team inside of the company, or to staff the PR function more modestly and rely primarily on one or more agencies. I am asked regularly which approach is better, but as with so many things in business, the answer depends on what you want from your PR team.

Having an internal team handle most – if not all – of your PR needs has several advantages, the most important of which is confidentiality. Companies whose release of information is exquisitely timed and that are subject to extraordinary levels of public scrutiny often choose to make PR an in-house affair. Apple is an excellent example.[1] Companies that rely on public relations as a primary marketing channel or that do a very high volume of PR work often find that it makes more sense to pay salaried employees than the hourly-based rates charged by agencies. Companies whose PR needs are predictable, controllable, and modest often opt to rely on one or two internal people to handle the work.

Why you shouldn't hire a PR agency in China

There are fair reasons not to hire a public relations agency in China, and you should take these into account before you consider taking the plunge.

PR agencies are expensive: Even if you work with a smaller, local agency, the way that the agency works is that they essentially charge you a substantial markup on the cost of their labor. If you are able to find the right people to staff an internal organization, you will wind up getting more man-hours for your dollar.

PR agencies don't know your business as well as you do: The most expert PR agencies are still outsiders to your company and your business, and bringing them up to speed is a time-consuming process.

Hiring a PR agency makes information less secure: Bringing an agency on board means having to share proprietary secrets, leaving the agency in a position to disclose sensitive information at critical times.

Hiring a PR agency is a costly, time-consuming process: Even if you are not bound by the strictures of a highly structured procurement process, it can take as long as two months and a lot of effort to hire an agency. It is entirely possible that your time is best spent elsewhere.

Why you should hire a PR agency in China

There are also a host of reasons that argue in favor of hiring a PR agency in China, including:

Scalable resources: A company's public relations' needs fluctuate throughout the year and over time. Hiring internally to address those needs can use up a valuable headcount that will either be underutilized, or can cause burnout because teams that are sized down will be overworked during high-intensity periods.

Outside point of view: China is a complex market, and there will be many times in a year when you will be glad to have an informed point of view from outside the organization to use as a sanity check. What is more, the agency should be able to provide insights from its experience across other industries.

Access to the bench: Most agencies are not an undifferentiated lump of PR people, but a unique mix of talents in a range of public relations sub-fields. It would not make sense to hire all of that talent, but having it on tap is essential.

Guarantee against personnel disruption: When you lose an internal PR person, you have a hole in your team. When an agency loses a person, that individual is usually replaced immediately, ensuring continuity of effort.

Fewer staffing challenges: If you have issues with an internal team member, getting rid of him or her can be a headache. Firing a PR agency is much more straightforward.

Hiring assistance: As noted in Chapter 1, finding talent can be difficult. Agencies can provide fill-in help while you are looking for people, and can usually even provide candidates for you to review and consider.

In the end, the choice revolves around whether having an outside agency suits your needs. For most companies whose needs are growing quickly and that have the need for flexibility or want access to a wide range of PR talent, hiring an agency is an easy choice.

How to hire a PR agency in China

Hiring a PR team can be time-consuming, costly, and, in China, extraordinarily difficult. As we noted in Chapter 1, the public relations industry in China has grown from a small base with great speed; companies are expanding their PR staff as challenges grow, and more Chinese firms are discovering that the public relations function is an essential part of a professional management team. This means that the demand for qualified PR people who understand the market and the industry far outstrips supply. Hiring just one qualified PR manager can be a challenge, even more so an entire internal team. For this reason, most companies opt to hire outside agencies, and in some cases will even hire an agency before they hire a local team.

Your process should begin with some basic research, doing Google or Baidu searches on PR firms with offices in the city you use as your China HQ. That should give you a fair initial picture of the kinds of agencies that would be of interest.

In addition, *The Holmes Report*, which reigns as the global public relations industry's trade publication of record, has over the past several years built a clear picture of the PR business in China, and invests heavily in being able to deliver an accurate assessment of the field of agencies. For a balanced idea of the agencies that matter – and would matter to you – *The Holmes Report* should be your second stop after the search engines.

Take the time to ask around people you know and trust. Who have they heard about? Who do they work with? Who is working for your competitors?

Once you have a general idea of the kind of agency you would like to work with, it is time to assemble your request for proposals (RFP). Make the RFP request as detailed as possible. Introduce your company and your business in China. Explain why you are looking for an agency, what you want that agency to do, and how it will fit into your overall PR team. If possible, provide a scope of work, and explain what you want presented. Finally, describe the criteria on which you will judge responses, and a calendar for the process. Send all this out with a deadline, and watch the proposals come in.

Your next task, and your most important, will be narrowing the field down to the agency that is the best fit for you. Keep in mind that when you hire an agency in China, whether or not you have to answer to a procurement process, you should be looking for several factors that will help determine whether the relationship (and hiring an agency *is* a relationship) will work out over time.

Chemistry: Are you comfortable with the team? Are they comfortable with you? Can you imagine working with them for an extended duration, perhaps in a crisis?

Competency: Do they have demonstrable competency in the areas you need help in? Do they appear to know what they are talking about, or are they bluffing their way through the discussion?

Creativity: New problems and challenges emerge constantly. You want an agency that is able to apply some basic creativity to some of those problems and build campaigns that are both engaging and interesting.

Capabilities: Do they only provide media relations services, or are they able to provide counsel and service across a wide range of public relations services?

Strategic planning: Are their capabilities purely executional, or do they demonstrably have the ability to think about PR at an enterprise level? Do you need strategic thinking, or just inexpensive execution?

Bench depth: Does the team seem fairly thin, or are there enough people with the right skills so that if someone was on vacation or sick they could still provide uninterrupted service?

Too many senior people in the pitch: This is usually a sign that they are stacking the pitch in order to win the business. Be wary of an agency that promises to bring the day-to-day people later – they may be hiding something and trying to dazzle you with experience in the process.

Minimal conflicts: Ideally the agency will have experience in your sector, but may not be servicing any competitors at the moment. If the agency is large enough, it should have no problem building a "Chinese wall" between client teams, but use caution – information flow is hard to contain within an office.

Integrity: Skilled people are easily hired in China, but challenge an agency to talk about integrity, and too often you get either blank stares or a defensive half-answer: "Why, yes, of course we have integrity. I just thought that would go without saying." It does not, and you should not hesitate to grill a prospective agency about what it thinks integrity is, and how it hires for it. These are, after all, people whom you are trusting with your brand and your reputation. You want those things in the hands of individuals who understand the difference between right and wrong and unfailingly choose right.

Knowledge of your industry: You are going to need to invest in an onboarding process with any PR agency (see "Managing a PR agency in China" below), but ideally you want to have to spend as little time as possible bringing your PR folks up to speed. Onboarding is an overhead and you will likely be paying for the time your agency people spend learning the business.

An understanding of business generally: It is a sad fact about public relations in China that most practitioners have come up through the narrow silo of PR, and most, if they comprehend the broader challenges of an enterprise at all, still see it through the prism of public relations. That can be a handicap. Most enterprises in China face public relations challenges with origins distant from the way that media perceive the company. PR issues are generally rooted in issues from other parts of the enterprise, and you want PR advisors who understand the full scope of the challenges you face in addressing those issues. Look for teams that are seasoned with practitioners from outside the pure PR fold: a client leader who has run her own business, has managed an in-house PR department, or who comes from a general management background are all big plusses; team members who were trained as attorneys, accountants or physicians, or who transferred from other functional areas will also help. What you are looking for is a group that draws from a wider swathe of experience than someone who studied PR in university and has been doing it ever since.

Adult supervision: Public relations in China essentially did not exist until the mid-1980s. In the three decades since, the craft has grown at double-digit rates every year. As a result, the makeup of the industry is exceedingly young. While in the United States you would rarely see a vice-president under 30 or a managing director under 35, in China it is depressingly common to see agency managing directors who are still in their 20s. Why "depressing?" Because, while there are certainly outstanding individuals who deserve such swift promotion, all too many of those young leaders have been denied the opportunity to develop the wisdom, gravitas, and breadth of knowledge and experience that will enable them to offer counsel on more than just their limited area of specialty. Granted, not every PR assignment demands the attention of a gray eminence. Nonetheless, having one either on the team or attached as senior adviser ensures that when you need the benefits of age and experience, they are ready at hand.

Global agency or best-of-breed? Global agencies, and especially the global majors, love worldwide assignments, so you are likely to be approached by big firms seeking an engagement that will have you conduct a single pitch for all markets globally. This makes great sense for the agency (it tends to offer a higher return on the investment made in pitching), and it also ensures that they can funnel business into operations around the world that house decent practitioners but have a hard time supporting themselves. If you need a public relations service worldwide, a global agency may indeed make much sense. As we have noted, pitching is expensive for the client as well as the agency.

This should serve as a basic checklist for your review process, helping you to pick out the agency that is not only the best prepared, but, more importantly, is the best suited to mesh with your team.

Managing a PR agency in China

Once you have hired a public relations agency, your challenge is to get the most out of that arrangement. In order to help you do this, I am going to break ranks with my fellow agency people and offer some politically incorrect advice; but if you heed it, I can promise that the money you spend on an agency will be money well invested rather than money wasted.

Invest in onboarding

You have been through an exhaustive process to hire what you believe to be the best agency available. The biggest mistake that you could make at this point is to neglect their early education. Given the importance of the China market, it is worth your while to spend between one and three days providing the team with a deep-dive into your business, what PR activities you have undertaken to date, what your challenges are, and what the calendar looks like for the year ahead.

If possible, arrange for the team to meet all of the China senior executives. They will also be working for them, and the better they know them, the more helpful the agency will be in the effort to build thought leadership products, quotes, and profiles of the executives.

Ideally, one or two of the most senior members of the team would travel to HQ with you to meet your counterparts. This eases the process of integrating the team, and you can be certain that within the first several months of working together you will have need for your agency and your colleagues to be in touch directly.

Keep in mind that even with the best onboarding process, the education of the agency will continue for months, so manage your expectations. The agency will have a lot to take in within a very short period of time, and experience remains the best teacher. Onboarding will give them a boost and make them productive from the outset.

Make your agency drive you

All too often in managing an agency you will find yourself chasing up after one thing and another. This is tiring, boring, and generally unnecessary. Make it clear to the agency from the start that you expect them to be reminding you about what they are doing and what you need to do to support them.

This role reversal is not an abdication of your responsibility. It is, however, a subtle invitation to the agency to take the initiative *in everything that they do*. The result for you should not only be that you don't need to chase up after every little thing; it will also produce an agency relationship wherein the agency is constantly coming to you with ideas and opportunities.

In short, by forcing the agency to drive you, you will wind up with an agency that is more strategic, more engaged, and more vested in your success.

Live by the client code of conduct

Finally, when you work with an agency, keep in mind that respect works both ways. In two decades in this business, I have witnessed some truly shameful behavior toward agencies – behavior that should actually be illegal.

Follow the simple rules below, and you will come out with a better working relationship with your agency – one filled with excitement and quality work rather than grudging passive-aggressive behavior.

- I will pay my bills as long as those bills reflect the terms of the contract and work done.

- I will pay those bills on time at the speed I expect to be paid for my own goods and services.
- I will not ask my service providers to engage in unethical or illegal practices.
- I will not re-negotiate my contract with the service providers while that service is being provided.
- I will do everything I can to ensure the service provider's success in its engagement with me.

* * *

That's a great place to end, because it leaves us on the most important theme of all.

Public relations in China will only be as successful as the team you build to conduct it. It is no coincidence that we began this book with a focus on building your internal team, and end it with a discussion about agencies. People are the bookends of a successful public relations program in China, and all of the plans, ideas, research, tactics, strategy, channels and tools mean precious little without engaged, passionate, motivated, and dedicated people.

In the end, what will make or break your brand in China are people – you need PR people who understand you and who understand this remarkable country. If I can leave you with one thought, it is this: the most important investment you will make in Chinese PR is the time you invest in your PR team.

Good luck!

Notes

Introduction

1. As you would expect, there is some hyperbole here, but not much. After I finished a talk about Chinese brands at a British Chamber of Commerce function in Beijing in 2012, I was buttonholed by a local executive who wanted to let me know that he didn't go in for this marketing and PR "stuff." As long as he had a sales team that worked, that was all he needed.

1   The Basics and First Steps

1. The term "guanxi" defies simple translation into English. Books can be (and have been) written about the concept. It is most often translated as "relationships," but what it really refers to is both the relationships that you have with people of power and influence *and* the set of mutual obligations that underpin those relationships according to Chinese custom.

2   Public Relations and the Chinese Government

1. China has at least five levels of government below the national level: provincial, prefectural, county, township, and village. Not all of these will be relevant to all companies at all times but it will be essential in

developing a public affairs plan that PA teams understand which of these are important and relevant, and which bureaus and agencies within each level have an interest in your business.

2. An excellent example of this was the 1998 merger of the Ministry of Posts and Telecommunications with the Ministry of Electronics industry to create the Ministry of Information Industries. Party officials in charge of propaganda had objected to the inclusion in that merger of the Ministry of Radio, Film, and Television and the State Administration of Press and Publications. In a fillip to that group, the media were excluded from the merger. The result was a decade of low-intensity bureaucratic warfare regarding which agency had jurisdiction over such fast-growing sectors as cable television and the internet, with businesses left to deal with the fallout.

3. Moving goods around China can be a challenge for many reasons; not least is the functional protectionism imposed by provinces and cities. Provinces have been known to impose the equivalent of tariffs on the "importation" of goods from other provinces that compete with their own industries, and even Beijing places deep restrictions on trucks and delivery vans from outside the city.

4. The first person I heard use the term "chorus of voices" was Susan Tomsett, when she referred to the strategy of building support among multiple domestic audiences in this way.

5. It is important to use caution when approaching local Chinese industry associations about the issue of policy advocacy. Many of these organizations are organized by the government as a means of exerting a higher degree of control over the activities of industries, or to head off the creation of independent associations that might become political players outside of the CCP fold. In some cases, the association with the government might prove an advantage, especially as senior officials may hold board positions in the association, and the organization may prove to be a forum you can use to forge the common cause. Nonetheless, use care and get lots of advice about the particular association before trying to mobilize it.

6. It should impress the reader that this relatively low standard of corporate citizenship is reflective of some significant deficiencies in these areas among local and foreign companies operating in China.

3   Working with the Media in China

1. See   http://www.slideshare.net/catchadigital/emarketer-worldwidead spendingforecast.
2. See http://cmp.hku.hk/2014/09/19/36099/
3. It is important to note that a small handful of media outlets continued to benefit from government largesse to ensure that the Party always had channels to the people. These outlets are believed to include China Central Television, Xinhua News Agency, China National Radio, and *The People's Daily.*

4   Public Relations and Corporate Change in China

1. For Carlyle's press release on the deal, see http://www.carlyle.com/news-room/news-release-archive/carlyle-group-agrees-acquire-85-stake-xugong-group-construction-machinery-
2. See http://www.thebeijingaxis.com/tca/editions/the-china-analyst-sep-2011/90-rising-stars-chinas-emerging-construction-machinery-manufacturers
3. See http://news.xinhuanet.com/english/2008-07/24/content_8760203. htm.
4. See   http://www.taipeitimes.com/News/worldbiz/archives/2006/08/04/2003321777
5. See   http://www.washingtonpost.com/wp-dyn/content/article/2007/03/29/AR2007032900780_pf.html
6. Here in Chinese on Sina.com: http://finance.sina.com.cn/chanjing/b/20080908/06485281183.shtml
7. See   http://blogs.wsj.com/chinarealtime/2008/09/10/coke-huiyuans-chinese-media-battle/?mod=googlenews_wsj
8. For the record, Coke learned much from the deal, and now makes something of a fetish about understanding the local policy environment. Full disclosure: I was asked to brief current CEO Muhtar Kent and his team in 2013 while Kent was serving as head of Coke's international operations.
9. See http://www.businessweek.com/globalbiz/content/mar2009/gb20090318_570130.htm

10. I go into detail in a blog post from the time here: http:// siliconhutong.com/2009/03/18/seven-reasons-for-the-coke-huiyuan-epic-fail/ There were a range of issues in the policy environment to suggest that both the timing of the deal and the selection of Huiyuan as a target were problematic.
11. See http://www.chinalawblog.com/2008/08/chinas_antimonopoly_law_people.html
12. Personal conversation between the author and Mr. Moss.
13. Simon Baxter, Frederic Depoortere, Andrew L. Foster, "China Merger Control: New Carrots and a Bigger Stick," *Skadden, Arps, Slate, Meagher & Flom LLP*, April 23, 2014. Retrieved March 6, 2015 from http://www.skadden.com/insights/china-merger-control-new-carrots-and-bigger-stick

5 Crisis Management in China

1. This is a heavy fictionalization of a crisis faced by a European white goods manufacturer. The hammers and the celebrities were real, and a great illustration of the kind of melodrama that often accompanies crisis in China.
2. Bill Snyder, "Snowden: The NSA planted backdoors in Cisco products," InfoWorld.com, May 15, 2014, retrieved May 6, 2015 from http:// www.infoworld.com/article/2608141/internet-privacy/snowden--the-nsa-planted-backdoors-in-cisco-products.html
3. Todd Rosene suggested this phrasing. My original words were: "It takes years to build a brand in China, but it only takes the minutes that you remain incommunicado in a crisis to destroy it." You choose the one you prefer.
4. This is precisely what happened to BP CEO Tony Hayward. In his defence, he was overworked and left himself on the front lines of the battle for too long. Admirable, but even the captain has to leave the bridge at some point, or the ship will wind up on the rocks.

6 Social Media and Public Relations in China

1. "Inside the War Against China's Blogs," *BusinessWeek*, June 11, 2008, retrieved March 6, 2015 from www.bloomberg.com/bw/stories/2008-06-11/inside-the-war-against-chinas-blogs

7 Conducting Effective PR in China

1. Zhao Hao, Chen Junyu and Liu Zhiqian, "Milking the Hype," *News China*, January 2011. Retrieved March 6, 2015 from www.newschinamag.com/magazine/milking-the-hype.
2. This section is heavily derived from my blog post "The Looming Crisis for Public Relations in China" http://siliconhutong.com/2010/11/01/the-looming-crisis-for-public-relations-in-china/.
3. The act, frequently called the FCPA (The Foreign Corrupt Practices Act), can be found in its full text in Section 78dd of Title 15 of the United States Code (15 U.S.C. § 78dd-1 et seq.)
4. Canada has the Corruption of Foreign Public Officials Act, and the United Kingdom has passed the Bribery Act, both to fulfill a similar purpose to the FCPA in the United States.

9 Public Relations Agencies in China

1. Three times in the past 14 years I have been approached by a PR manager new to Apple who wanted to engage my firm, only to have to withdraw the offer when told that the company does not engage agencies.

Index